"This is a beautifully sensual account of the sights, sounds, smells, tastes, and emotions entailed in daily life on a Tennessee farm, very lovingly rendered with gratitude for being in a place worth caring about."
    —**James Howard Kunstler**, author of the *World Made by Hand* novels

"I've long been an admirer of Brian Miller's writing, and I hope this delightful book will find him many new readers. With perfect authorial control, it combines lyricism, self-deprecating humor, a grounding in place, political wisdom that's all the more powerful for its understatement, and deep practical knowledge from a life on the land. A book to be read and enjoyed, but also—more unusually—to be acted upon."
    —**Chris Smaje**, author of *Saying No to a Farm-Free Future*

"What a beautiful and inspiring book! Brian Miller has given us a wonderful meditation on the glories and difficulties of life on his well-ordered East Tennessee farm. Chronicled according to the liturgy of the hours, Miller reminds us of the importance of learning 'to walk and not run though the seasons.' It is rich in both literary allusion and sober practical advice. *Kayaking with Lambs* is a celebration of the archaic arts, the joy of duty, and the rich rewards of the habit of attention."
    —**Scott H. Moore**, author of *How to Burn a Goat*

"From the taste of a fat blackberry on a warm afternoon to 'the sound of the moon rising' to the sweet smell of lamb poop, Brian Miller conveys the small joys, alongside the modern perplexities, of shepherding a small farm. His attention to the cycles of life, of the seasons, and of each day transforms his 'farm notes' into a form of poetry."
    —**Allan Carlson**, author of *The New Agrarian Mind*

"Good books about farm life and rural community are rare to say the least. Great books are rarer still. In *Kayaking with Lambs*, Brian Miller has accomplished the latter. Arranged as daily meditations, Miller takes readers on a delightful journey of his working farm, baring his heart and soul in the process. Along the way, we meet a menagerie of farm animals, as well as his best and sometimes not-so-good neighbors. A fantastic read."
    —**Donald E. Davis**, author of *Where There Are Mountains*

Kayaking with Lambs

Kayaking with Lambs

Notes from an East Tennessee Farmer

BRIAN D. MILLER

Front Porch Republic *Books*

KAYAKING WITH LAMBS
Notes from an East Tennessee Farmer

Resource Publications
An Imprint of Wipf and Stock Publishers
199 W. 8th Ave., Suite 3
Eugene, OR 97401

www.wipfandstock.com

PAPERBACK ISBN: 978-1-6667-8167-0
HARDCOVER ISBN: 978-1-6667-8168-7
EBOOK ISBN: 978-1-6667-8169-4

VERSION NUMBER 081523

To Cindy, for everything

Canticle of the Sun

Be praised, my Lord, through all your creatures,
especially through my lord Brother Sun,
who brings the day; and you give light through him.
And he is beautiful and radiant in all his splendor!
Of you, Most High, he bears the likeness.

Praised be You, my Lord, through Sister Moon and the stars,
in heaven you formed them clear and precious and beautiful.

Praised be You, my Lord, through Brother Wind,
and through the air, cloudy and serene,
and every kind of weather through which
You give sustenance to Your creatures.

Praised be You, my Lord, through Sister Water,
which is very useful and humble and precious and chaste.

Praised be You, my Lord, through Brother Fire,
through whom you light the night and he is beautiful
and playful and robust and strong.

Praised be You, my Lord, through Sister Mother Earth,
who sustains us and governs us and who produces
varied fruits with colored flowers and herbs.

Praised be You, my Lord,
through our Sister Bodily Death,
from whom no living man can escape.

—St. Francis of Assisi

I

Matins

THE OFFICE BEGINS AT *midnight at the top of the hill on a cold March night. The hour opens in long silence with the taste of snow in the steady wind. The few lights from our kith down in the valley seem more intimate for their distance. Signaling the presence of a modern life alone, they are connected and affirmed by the grid of power lines humming a feeble supremacy on the far edge of the pasture.*

Overhead, through gaps in the cloud curtain, the sharp clarity of winter stars is visible in the night sky, remote intelligences communicating in a winking semaphore the unwelcome message of humility and insignificance. From my chair, my feet firm on the pasture, I hear behind me what must be a rabbit breaking cover, pursued by my dogs, conveying in their own language a place and hierarchy.

The owls hoot from the twenty-acre wood beyond me a song of plausible deniability as the rabbit escapes under a fence and back to ground. On a nearby ridge coyotes yip a prayer for sustenance. The hens shift on their roost and squawk a nervous call and response, a sound of apprehension carried up the hill to my ears. The world in acts, some played and some still being written, surrounds in this hour. The challenge comes in a quiet listening beyond my own thoughts.

I break the hour and pick up my chair and return down the hill. My boots make small crackling sounds on the frozen ground, and a few swirling snowflakes accompany me with a delicate dance. Each step brings me closer to home and further away from my reverie.

A last glance skyward, before I enter the house, finds the semaphore code broken as the clouds shutter the sky. The world is once again close in and yet remote, both knowable and unknown. The link now only a thread, I open the door.

Midnight skies, a flock of wild turkeys heard but not seen on the opposing ridge. The uncontrollable spread of wild mint, the delicate blossoms of peach trees in bloom, the muscle ache from setting thirty fence posts. My giddy delight as I stand back and admire our newly built equipment shed, the morning sun when it throws a splash of color through the Victorian stained-glass window into the tack shed. Collecting fruits from a wild persimmon to make beer, not knowing or caring what it will taste like. Breathing in the sweet fragrance of hay drying in the field on a hot summer evening, approaching warily in an attempt to move an irascible bull, gentling a rooster before butchering. A wake of buzzards perched high in a skeletal tree, staring down at me as I sweat in the garden, their black eyes shiny with expectation and hope. Standing in the shadows of the barn sometime between midnight and dawn, watching in silence while I wait for Daisy to calve. These are some of the reasons I farm.

A late-dawn walk finds me down the lane behind the house, a four-acre woodlot to my right. On my left, screened by a copse, is a long pasture that slopes up the hill to the east. At the far end of the lane lies a massive fallen oak, straddling the two worlds. I sit on the trunk with my collie-heeler, Tip, and watch the sun rise on one of my favorite views.

The pasture is smooth, clear of any obstruction, rock, or tree. The grass is short and green, covered with a thick sheen of white crystals left from Jack Frost's nightly visit. The field undulates in folds and curves, presenting a starkly sensual portrait as the sun rises and illumines through leafless trees select contours of the land.

The blankets of frost quickly disappear in streaks where the sun touches the hill. In minutes the pasture is rippled with stripes of green. It will be another hour before the sun vanquishes the frost from the pastures, another hour yet before all that remains of a cold night is the skim of ice on water troughs and the crunch of grass in the shade of the porch.

At the desk where I write, my view is of the chicken yard and coop. The light has crested the hill and hits the coop window, a window of ancient and honorable pedigree. A rectangular piece of zinc-lined glass as tall as I am, each pane is four inches square of distorted waves from a pre-mass-production furnace. The window is one of a handful rescued from the turn-of-the-twentieth-century Jacob Building at Chilhowee Park in Knoxville, Tennessee, after it burned in the late thirties. The remnant of a grand palace of a now-vanished agricultural heritage, it gives reflected light to our hens on their roosts.

I stand in our oldest orchard, where the light is provided by the full moon. High and staggered clouds pass across the sky, presenting a stop-and-go slide show with the moonlight. The loud cough of a buck on the hill beyond the orchard signals a failed attempt to cross above me discreetly. Now that hunting season is almost upon us, the deer are moving at night more than in the daylight. They know the time for prudence is now. On opening day we will be greeted by a barrage of gunfire at sunrise.

I reach out in the darkness and grab a scuppernong vine and give it a shake. Overripe grapes fall into the wet grass like large, soft, heavy raindrops. Walking back down the slope through the orchard, past the equipment shed, I close the door to the chicken run. The noise causes the hens to stir. They wheeze and shift and go back to sleep.

The pounding of a hammer and the clanking of clamps, and I know Cindy is in the workshop. She is building a floor-to-ceiling kitchen cupboard with glass doors. The occasional expletive signals a perfectionist's ongoing struggle with a project that has to be well done. I, on the other hand, can scrape the bark off a branch, call it a walking stick, and be absurdly pleased.

I lean across the fence and breathe in the lambs. The sweet smell of wet wool and the poop of an animal that eats only forage rises up out of the pasture. Lambs have quiet and meek little bleats. Their soft tread in the grass is just audible as they are torn between curiosity and alarm at my presence.

I reach down, tear off, and then wad up a turnip green in my mouth. The dark green leaf offers a wonderful explosion of spice, all mustard with the texture of a tobacco leaf. I turn back toward the house. All three dogs vie for the honor of walking by my side. They snarl and fight. Robby wins and heels by my left leg as I walk up the steps.

✣

The first gate leading into the large wooded pig paddock hangs next to a building we call "the other house." One of the few structures on our farm when we bought this land in 1999, it is the size and configuration of a three-bay garage, with two of the three "bays" fully enclosed as rooms. The previous owner had built the structure, but he felt cooped up on seventy acres in East Tennessee and headed to Montana before moving forward with a more permanent residence. We finished out two of the bays for a living space, where we stayed for three years while we expanded the farm's infrastructure and then built a home of our own.

The eight-foot gate next to the building leads into an alleyway with two other gates, all of which facilitates the loading of pigs. It is through this chute system that I pass on a Saturday afternoon with no aim but a ramble with a cigar. Ahead some thirty feet is a pig trough, where fat, grain-fed squirrels cluster around the remains of a porcine feast. The massive barrows are deeper in the woods, taking a postprandial siesta. At the clang of the gate the rodents are off. They struggle to heft their bulk up an oak tree and out of sight.

This wooded paddock is markedly different from the open woods beyond. It is more rocky moonscape than lush landscape. Pigs will do that to the land. In the past fifteen years the hogs we've raised on this parcel have gradually thinned out the brush and the smaller trees, leaving in their wake only a few sprigs of grass and enough debris to please a tornado. I cross the one-acre paddock and enter into a 50-by-200-foot enclosure on the far side. There the remains of a twelve-port wooden hog feeder lie unused and in disrepair. A skulking rat scurries past my periphery but is gone before I can turn my head. I pull out my little notebook and jot down, "Clean up feeder." Time to get our own debris out of these woods.

In the middle of the enclosure stands a woebegone maple, three feet in diameter. The base is rotted and has been hollowed out by the hogs. *Someday, maybe sooner than later, a pig in search of grubs will be in for a surprise,* I think.

Across the fence is a clean five-acre field belonging to one of our closest neighbors, a young couple. The man and I agreed a few weeks back, while cutting up a large fallen oak, that I would harvest the field this year for hay for our farm. The area has not been pastured seriously in all the time we have been on this land, and I hope for a good yield. That cutting plus cuttings from our lower seven acres should pack the hay barns from floor to rafters.

The flight of half a dozen whitetails through the brush turns my gaze. While I have pondered over my future forage wealth, the deer, who heretofore have been watchful, finally feel it prudent to move on, and at speed. White flags flipping through the undergrowth, quick sprints and then a pause, a few more steps, an effortless sail over barbed wire at the far end of this patch of woods, and they are gone. Walking back I make more notes of possible projects. I stop and scratch the sleeping hogs along the way. They have three months left on this earth before providing an excellent return in bacon and pork chops to us and our customers.

Just over the fence from where I now stand is our twelve-acre hill pasture. I spent this morning subdividing it into half-acre grazing paddocks separated by electric fencing. While we don't rotate our flock of mostly Katahdin sheep as often as some, we do more than most. Every two weeks they move on to a new section of green grass, at least in seasons of fast growth. I'll turn them into a new paddock in the morning. Much like pigs, sheep do an effective job of keeping the land cleared—perhaps too effective: leave too many of them too long, and our hills may begin to resemble those of Greece. So it's critical to keep them on the move, again and again.

I turn and walk back to the house and put on our afternoon pot of coffee.

The furnace was fine, not in fact burning the house down. I knew firsthand, because I had spent the last forty-five minutes, flashlight gripped in my right hand, slithering on my belly in and out of tight spots, inspecting the ductwork under the house. I had also checked the new HVAC unit outside, laid hands on various components, stuck my head in close and smelled. All seemed fine.

That I had done all of this in the middle of the night I can only chalk up to love. As in, "Brian, there is a noise downstairs." Or, as in this case, upon being nudged awake at two o'clock with, "Do you smell that? It smells like something is burning." Whereupon, message delivered, the beloved turns over and falls immediately back into sweet dreams.

Eyes now open, ill humor and sleep a memory fogged by urgent thoughts of what to grab first, I get out of bed, dress, and begin to inspect, one by one, all the possible flashpoints. *No, I do not and never did smell something burning.* But I persevere. As they say, in for a penny. . . . Which is why at just after three o'clock I emerge from the crawlspace under the house, straighten, and glance toward the sky.

Cold night skies have a clarity that even with the distant lights of towns on the horizon move me to pause in reverence. I stand there and gaze at the vastness of the Milky Way splashed in a long arc above. Hidden in the shadow of earth, the moon is blood red, only the smallest sliver of pearl white lighting an edge. The goodnight moon of bedtime is now fully into a lunar eclipse.

I'm not sure how long I stand, dressed in dirty coveralls, pads strapped to my knees, flashlight in hand, just staring. Every few minutes I look around, hoping for someone or something with whom to share the awe. "Do you see this? Is this not spectacular?" I whisper. But I am alone. The infinite sky and the ancient moon teach the same old lessons in humility I've learned and forgotten so many times, that even with the mistakes I make with my life, in this merest blink of existence, the universe is eternal and offers countless opportunities to get it right, somewhere, that perhaps we are just incidental to the plan.

It is four in the morning before I come back in the house. I put on a pot of coffee, sleep no longer on the agenda, grab my camera, and go back out to take a few shots. I'm not sure why I feel the need to document what was a spiritual, literally otherworldly, moment, but it is what we do in this modern life. As I stand on the porch, two shooting stars burn a brief trail into the atmosphere and are gone.

It is the kind of drive that restores some of my dwindling supply of faith. On this late spring day, two kids in inner tubes are bobbing in the faster current of Cedar Fork Creek where it sweeps under the bridge over Possum Trot. Cedar Fork is an unremarkable stream that runs alongside our road, and it never builds up much speed unless in flood. I honk my horn in hello as I pass. Across the way a neighbor is using a skid steer to smooth out a new driveway. He looks up and waves.

The skies are May blue, with deeper shades and depths in the distance where storms linger without threat. I make the left turn onto Ross Road. In a small pasture on the right that stretches to a low wooded ridge a large family works together to set out a garden. The man tills while his teenage sons pull sod from the patch. Back a distance from the road a cluster of women chat in the shade. Perched in lawn chairs next to another section of the creek, they keep a close eye on a passel of youngsters who run shrieking in and out of the water in a game of chase.

Around the curve I brake suddenly for a flock of chickens crossing. They belong to a neighbor whose poultry roam at will during daylight hours, as they should on all winding country lanes. That I never see a dead chicken in the road shows that either the poultry are street savvy or at least that area drivers keep a sharp watch. Off to the side of the neighbor's is a six-by-eight-foot homemade hoop-house. Behind it, in a quarter-acre lot, a distinctive pod of hogs lies beached under the cool shade of overhanging trees.

I glance to the left, where Big Sandy cuts off on an asphalt tributary. A man feeds his horses and another stacks firewood. Ross Road follows a soft curve, framed by the never-run-dry Cooley Spring to the left and a bulk feed bin to the right. Cresting the hill I see off behind a well-maintained ranch-style home that the wife of a fellow who has dug several ponds on our farm is taking her rest from mowing. We both wave.

Ross takes a long upward bend to the east just after passing Lynn Road to the south. I come upon another family that periodically buys our feeder pigs. They have recently leveled an old barn (which with the next good gust of wind would probably have fallen on its own), and today some of them are busy preparing the foundation for a replacement. Others are hoeing in an adjacent, embarrassingly tidy garden. Knowing the state of my own garden plot, I am tempted not to make eye contact, but they flip me a quick wave, and I reply in kind.

The road narrows as it passes through a wood just before a dairy. Upon emerging from the trees, the lane aligns at certain times of the year with both the rising sun and the eastward route of the morning school bus—making for a dangerous game that involves squinting and a desperate hope that your own vehicle and that of the bus driver are both in separate lanes, keeping all of us on the above-ground side of life.

The path widens slightly, and I turn down a hill between two dairy pastures, where I see the dairyman's wife tending the modest (and again tidy) garden across from her home. Another curve, past the dairy's calving paddock, alongside the milking parlor, and I'm on the final stretch to Stockton Valley.

At the stop sign I turn left. There's a large garden just behind a one-story red barn that sports an extensive collection of metal farm equipment signs. There's also a freshly baled hayfield and another brick rancher whose lawn is erupting with spring flowers. I've arrived at my boundary. I pick up speed on the long, quiet straightaway that leads out of our community.

Even after so many years of farming, each late July and August still finds me making notes on the doldrums, winds slack in the sails, waiting for that first sign of a change in the course of the weather. Knowing another six weeks of the same is ahead, I continue to find it hard to muster the energy for even basic tasks on the to-do list.

The dogs are more useless than I. Tip stretches out on the porch or behind the hydrangea and sleeps away the days of her dotage. Becky, having given birth to ten puppies seven weeks back, spends her time slipping from tree to tree in a furtive attempt to elude the heat and the grasping mouths of her offspring.

Meanwhile, in these long days after Robby's death last fall, Tip's old age, and Becky's maternity leave, the varmints and deer have decided that a banquet on the farm is in order. We lost all our spring chicks to skunks before I managed to relocate three of them to the afterlife. Rabbits gambol in easy reach of the snoozing Tip. If awake, she would feel the scorn directed at her diminished abilities. Instead, she sleeps through the evidence of her decline, legs twitching as she chases down the culprits in her dreams. (*Gibelotte de lapin*, my dear rabbits. Enjoy your salad days, for I will have mine and soon.)

Waking from my own midsummer's afternoon nap, I stroll into the kitchen to find a large doe in the backyard. "Becky, do your #$%@ing job!" I shout out the door. No reply. The doe grazes in the grapevines before languidly sailing over the fence and easing back to the woods. Becky ventures out of hiding just long enough for the ten puppies to spy her, waddle forth en masse, and attach like leaches. Her gaze turns to me, reproach and accusation evident in her eyes.

A fast-moving cold front left us with three inches of rain yesterday and a wonderfully cool morning today. I lace up my boots, grab my walking stick and a cup of coffee, and head into the woods for a morning stroll. An early morning ramble without a particular destination is always a great way to greet a new day, week, or year.

Large dew-covered spider webs grace the fence over the pig paddock. I look carefully while passing but discern no decipherable message in the weaving. I enter through the gates leading from the orchard to the pastures, then stroll along the fencerow separating the barn field from the upper field, Becky at my side. The cattle lumber down from the top of the hill toward me with an expectation that goes unfulfilled.

Once in the woods I follow the meandering forest lane. It wends for more than a quarter of a mile up to the back acreage. The sunlight is just starting to cascade over the ridge, and it spills out into the woods. Shafts of light layer above my head like rock strata, or a cathedral window carefully positioned to optimize sunlight.

Becky startles a doe from her morning repose and later trees a squirrel. The sunlight is penetrating deeper into the woods, creating minor eclipses as a tulip poplar and white oak cast their shadows across the face of the sun. I ascend the lane to the back pastures. Standing at the edge for a moment, balanced between light and shade, I turn back toward the coolness.

I am keeping my eye out for a pawpaw tree. Last night we dined at a friend's cabin on the edge of the Cherokee National Forest. As we walked along the creek bed at the base of the mountain before dinner, we spotted a cluster of wild pawpaw trees and feasted on their fallen fruit, a first for me. The pawpaw is our temperate climate's only native "tropical" fruit. It tastes like a cross between a banana and mango. We left that evening having secured permission to transplant several small seedlings. I had hoped to find pawpaws on our land during my morning stroll, but, unsuccessful, I turn my feet toward home. Back down the forest lane, across the spring-fed stream and into the barn pasture I go, Becky still by my side. I arrive at the barnyard and do the morning chores, then head back to the house, where Cindy has a bowl of oatmeal waiting for me.

❧

Somewhere on the long bypass around Kansas City, the pair of Red Devon bull calves have had enough. They had loaded easily that morning, when the seller met me in a mall parking lot. I had driven eleven hours to get the calves. Now, only an hour into the drive home, they are trying to climb out the back of the trailer through an opening sized to allow a horse or cow to stare at the passing traffic. I make an emergency stop on the eastern side of KC, find a farm supply store, and buy a panel of hog fencing. With the help of loaner bolt cutters, I trim the panel to fit the opening and put an end to the escape escapades.

If you farm or have a homestead, you have your own catalog of livestock transport stories, because if you have an urge to acquire stock, or an urgent need to move them, you will use whatever conveyance is most readily at hand, whether trailer, truck, car, wheelbarrow, or lead and halter. To haul animals is to give full scope for the unpredictable to happen with predictable regularity, as when a friend who was hauling a load of hogs to slaughter had his truck break down . . .

On I-40.

At rush hour.

In downtown Nashville.

Boy, did I laugh long and hard as he told his story. I knew firsthand that if a trailer is going to develop a terminal malfunction, it is not going to happen in the driveway. Rush hour in a large city on one of the busiest interstates in the country under a tight deadline—yep, that sounds most likely.

At the outbreak of Covid the hog industry was faced with processors closing and the consequent backlog and ultimate collapse of the complex chain of farrowing and finishing pigs destined for the supermarket and the nonexistent restaurant trade. Small farms like ours were sometimes the beneficiaries of panicking meat customers and panicking mass meat producers. One man in our area packed his large cattle trailer with weaned piglets he bought in Kentucky from one of the giant farrowing operations. He drove around the Southeast, stopping at strategic places to sell to small farmers and homesteaders. He sold hundreds of weanlings a week before the industrial machine began to sort out the bottleneck.

Cindy bought three piglets for our farm and three more for friends and neighbors. She hauled them in her hatchback, between the rear seat

11

and the back door. Good idea—no need to hook up the trailer for six twenty -pound weanlings, except . . . ten minutes into the twenty-minute drive home, those piglets, which apparently had been holding their sphincters tight since Kentucky, decided to let loose. Over the next month, every time we decided to head off the farm, Cindy would open her mouth to ask the question and I would hasten an answer before it was voiced: "Let's take my truck." Because pig shit lingers. Oh, does it linger.

I've hauled geese home from North Carolina in a rental car. I've hauled them from Ohio in the passenger seat of my truck. Cindy has hauled goats, newly purchased rams, and healthy and injured ewes (not mentioning pigs again) in her assorted hatchbacks and SUVs over the years. We have each driven to the post office half a dozen times to collect ducklings, goslings, and chicks.

All of this is on my mind Friday morning when the phone rings. Our postmistress is on the line. "Your geese are here," she says. I jump in my truck and drive the fifteen miles to our post office in the sprawling burg of Philadelphia, population 808. At the counter the chirps of baby poultry from multiple boxes make conversation and concentration difficult. This time of year it is air travel (fittingly) that seems to be the preferred method for transporting birds. By shouting, I communicate why I'm here, take ownership of the cardboard box of our goslings, which were shipped from New Mexico the day before, and escort them to the farm by back road, this time without incident.

My drive to the garbage dump in Paint Rock is a mere four and half miles. This day our rat terrier, Buster, rides shotgun on the console of the truck. We both gaze at the cloudless spring day outside. I pull past the Baptist church, then the volunteer firehall, and I see that the little corner market next to the dump is doing a thriving business in the exchange of children. The parking lot is one of those rural designated drop points where surly estranged parents offload their offspring for the weekend. But the failures of the formerly conjoined are not what is on my mind. I'm thinking instead of another spring, one that led me to this farming life twenty-some years ago.

While I have attributed my desire to farm to the influences of authors like James Herriot, I could credit the agrarian models of family as well. One of my grandfathers farmed rice and cattle before the Great Depression in

Louisiana's Acadia Parish. Another oversaw a pecan plantation in Beauregard Parish, near the town of Rosepine.

My farming journey also got a heady boost in the nineties, during another glorious East Tennessee spring, one spent delivering meals to rural shut-ins. I was marking time between jobs and volunteered to do daily lunch dropoffs to the elderly. Each morning I'd load hot meals into my pickup and head out to the more sparsely populated areas of Knox County. The recipients lived in tidy, humble homes, almost all with vegetable gardens, often with a half-dozen chickens scratching in the dust or a hog near the shed. Without exception, the occupants would cheerfully greet me on my arrival. One ninety-year-old woman was routinely in her woodshed splitting wood. Upon spotting me she would swing her axe into a large chunk of firewood, wipe her hands on her dress, then approach me with a friendly hello and collect her lunch.

During those few months I delivered meals, I watched the season unfold in such lovely and minute detail that I was ultimately seduced. The experience shifted my gaze from my trafficked city life and opened a door I wasn't aware I had wanted to enter. The evident contentment of my charges, the blossoming spring landscape, the loving care of those humble places—all of it moved me. Likewise, leaving those winding country roads for the city's sprawl and congestion made me want to heave the wheel and turn back around.

When my oldest sister died at the age of fifty-six, I flew to the family home in Lake Charles, Louisiana. That Monday evening after her death and through the next Friday on the day of her service saw a constant parade of neighbors and friends bringing platters of food into the house. Each evening cars began to show up, laden with casseroles, fried chicken, roast pork, boudin, banana puddings, salads, and cakes of all descriptions.

Visitors stayed for only minutes, long enough to voice their condolences, a show of respect for my sister and my family.

Those groaning tables of food lightened the grief, even made festive the gathering, and allowed the extended family to take communion over a shared meal. How often does it happen in our lives that the best memories are centered on a symbolic breaking of bread? It's an echo of our agrarian past, a statement that if we have food on the table we can weather any storm, that we can shelter in place until the danger has passed.

The average American moves 11.5 times in a lifetime. I moved thirteen before settling on the farm at age thirty-seven. These past years of staying put have been an education in how to be part of a place. The act of being a steward of this farm has made me more highly value the ties that bind us in life, those of community, neighbors, family, and land. I hope that has made me a more thoughtful custodian of those ties, but it's a determination I'll leave to those who know me best.

Every day that I plow through my long to-do list binds me tighter to this place. Each task completed makes me more a part of the farm, value more my nearby neighbors and distant family. While there are plenty of ways to fracture a community, neighbors, and family, as with the land, all can be nourished back into productivity with a little water, manure, and sunshine. Once again productive, if lightly used they can be lightly harvested. If nourished well they will thrive. If ignored and not cultivated, they wither.

Ultimately, we do give so we can receive. That is part of the compact of a healthy society and healthy land. And if we have done our part, we will reap the rewards: Our community will honor our survivors with food and honest sympathy. The land will honor us by continuing to offer food to those who come after. And, hopefully, if the life has been lived well, there will be a platter of banana pudding somewhere on the table.

They are right where I left them, sitting on top of a post—just one more of the distracted farmer's hazards of setting gloves, fence pliers, coffee mugs, or in this case a pair of binoculars, in an easily visible spot, then walking off and forgetting them. I am halfway back from the barn this morning when I recall where I had placed them the previous day.

The horizon is already rimmed with a rose pink that quickly fades into the darker blues of the predawn night. Still shining bright, Venus, poised over the house, serves as my pole star. The morning's rounds of checking the ewes reveal no new lambs since Cindy's midnight visit the night before, when she discovered the newly born twins of a Dorper/Katahdin cross. She moved the twins into a lambing pen, to spend the first twenty-four hours alone with their mother before being introduced to the chaos of the larger flock. Sequestering in a stall provides an opportunity for ewe and lambs to bond, as well as ensures that the newborns get colostrum, the high-nutrient first milk, and allows us to spot any signs of problems.

Just after lunch I return to check the ewes on winter pasture. Earlier in the morning I had unrolled a round hay bale across the field as part of my usual chores. The flock has spent the past few hours with noses buried in forage, and on my return the pregnant ewes, those already with lambs, and the unbred yearlings are now sprawled throughout the outer corral, satiated and chewing on cud. All but one, that is.

One ewe remains in the lower part of the field. The day is sunny, the temperature twenty-eight degrees with little wind—ideal lambing weather. The ewe had been standing off to herself at feeding earlier in the day, typically but not always a telltale sign that lambing is imminent. Now, as I watch from a hundred yards away, in the blink of an eye, a lamb shoots out and onto the ground.

Opening the gates, I slip through and walk gingerly down the hill, stopping about a hundred feet from the ewe. She has already gotten to work licking a good-size lamb, who soon stands on wobbly legs. I sit down to watch as the mother, after some minutes, nudges the little one back to the ewe's udder. This time, though, the mother won't stand still long enough for her baby to suckle. Every minute she gives a great heave, starting from the shoulders and rippling all the way to her hindquarters. Following each mighty contraction, she spins around, looking intently to see if she has missed something on the ground. Ten minutes on, about the time I've begun to feel some slight concern, she abruptly lies down and shoots out another lamb onto the cold ground. The freshly emerged twin gives a few convulsive twitches of life.

The next few minutes are both comical and alarming. The firstborn, still trying to nurse, shuffles around for better purchase. In the process, it manages to stand atop its oblivious sibling. Meanwhile, the mother shows no inclination to clean the newest-born, who continues to give an occasional twitch. The wobbly lamb standing finally topples over onto its sibling and in doing so is smeared afresh in the afterbirth of the second lamb, still lying on the ground. The ewe takes her maternal cue and dutifully and energetically begins licking the first (again) and encouraging it to nurse.

The one still on the ground doesn't move and is ignored. I trust most ewes to know instinctively what to do, and this is an experienced mother of multiple seasons. Nonetheless, I get up and approach the trio. I stoop and pick up a handful of fresh hay. The second-born lamb remains covered in the mucus of birth. I stand it on its feet and, using the fresh hay as my cloth, begin vigorously scrubbing it down. The mother, at this point, takes matters into hand and begins licking the lamb clean herself.

Both twins are by now standing, so I back away and leave the ewe to do her job. A couple of hours later I grab my binoculars and return to the top of the field. Mother and twins are still at the bottom, a hundred yards away, near the fence adjoining the lower hayfield. The lambs are up and nursing. Because I am hundreds more feet away in the opposite direction from the nearest water, I determine it best to go ahead and move the new family to a stall in the barn, where I can feed and water the ewe and keep an eye on the threesome. I place the binoculars on the fence post, once again go through the gates, head down the hill, and pick up the lambs.

Walking backwards, I inch uphill and into the barn, lambs in hand and mother following, leaving all three safely in a stall with fresh hay, a small handful of grain, and a bucket of clean water.

The next morning the pair of binoculars, other than sporting a fresh coat of frost, have weathered the night just fine, available again when I should need to spot a problem—or in this case, no problem—in a lower field in lambing season.

We are, by nature, a peripatetic people—we have been ever since we walked out of Africa millennia ago. Nonetheless, considering our countless generations of mass migrations as peoples, we remain devoted to the idea of home. We aspire to be part of something, as Wes Jackson would say, to be "native to this place."

One day, after a full morning of work, we take a drive to the tiny town of Spring City. We leave our farm for the relatively short trip of twenty-four miles. Passing the dam on the Tennessee River, in the shadows of the cooling towers at the Watts Bar Nuclear Plant, we arrive in Spring City by mid-afternoon.

Word has reached us that the much-missed vegetable market in Sweet-water that closed has reopened in Spring City (or perhaps, unbeknownst to us, the open-air had always had sister markets in both locations). In any case, we find the Spring City market tucked away on a narrow back street. I am looking for a local source for a couple of pounds of turnip seed. Cindy is hoping to pick up some flowering bushes. The owners offer a modest early spring assortment of plants, seeds, and vegetables, and we come away with a flat of twenty-five Red Acre cabbage starts and a handful of forsythia sprigs.

Last fall we lost four hives of bees. We first saw it as a failure on our part. We still do, but the recrimination has lessened as we've learned of countless losses by other area beekeepers during the same period. Not having bees at the moment has left us without any honey, so while at the vegetable market we ask the proprietors if they have any from a local apiary. They both shake their heads. No local honey, they tell us, then point to what they do have to offer. I pick up a jar of honey, the label of which lists it as produced by a beekeeper in Sweetwater . . . thirty miles across the valley.

In an era of trade that spans our massive planet, this jar of honey—sourced thirty miles away and sitting on a shelf on the North American continent in the eastern part of one of our fifty states, in a large valley, the distance between two small towns that are in essence neighbors—is deemed "not local." While some might consider that parochial, I consider it hopeful.

In the vast scheme of time our movements have covered the globe. But our view is still constrained by the horizon and our lifespan. Our needs remain personal and consistent, native to our own place in the history of migrations. And maybe that is enough.

A while back I spent a couple of days in the heartland. I flew into the Indianapolis airport and then took Highway 36 from Indiana into the middle of Illinois. A two-lane road as straight as a plumb line, it takes you through some of the richest agricultural land in this country. Small towns are planted every five to ten miles, and even an oddly placed subdivision pops up in what seems the middle of nowhere amid vast oceans of farmland.

Having nothing better to do with my time, I counted vegetable gardens. I counted as I drove through towns on the highway. I counted as I passed those subdivisions, as I passed farms by the dozens. Finishing the trip two and half hours later, I had spotted a grand total of zero vegetable plots. Recent digs at my neighbors for not planting gardens now seem misplaced, because well over half of the homes in our valley have at least some sort of vegetable garden.

But zero?

Now we can assume I missed plenty. But I was diligent in looking, and even a casual survey should have turned up the odd patch of tilled ground behind a house or two. But I also didn't see any small orchards or grapevines, while most homes in our valley sport at least a pear tree or two in the front yard.

What could account for a food desert in this landscape? Was this the curse of rich land and commodity prices? Or was it that I was simply looking at 200 miles of an industrial park disguised as an agrarian landscape— a bit like those fake Hollywood towns of yore: they look the look at first glance, but there ain't nothing past the front wall.

It was odd to see old farmhouses with the corn and soybeans tilled and planted up to the driveways, the houses bobbing on the landscape like boats lost at sea. Gone were the outbuildings and barns of our history, now replaced with corrugated buildings housing supplies and gargantuan equipment. No room in this landscape for the personal or something as humble as a vegetable patch or fruit tree. No need for the homestead pig or grapevine. The message was clear: this is valuable land.

Yet what explained the absence in towns of vegetable gardens? As is my wont, I'm no doubt guilty of reading too much into this simple lack of observable gardens. But vegetable gardens, a few chickens, and a fruit tree or two make a statement. Their absence in our rich heartland is also a statement, a darker one, I think, a yielding of one's will or culture to other forces. Perhaps it is better to farm or garden on land that requires a bit more struggle?

2

Lauds

THE DAWN OFFICE IS *taken at five in the morn in the cool canopy of the old orchard. It is an ending of the night and a start to the new day, the work ahead still unformed, drifting through my mind like the mists in the creek bottoms below the farm. The third-quarter moon presides over the southern late winter sky, one eye on the job in front and one eye on the job completed. The Big Dipper holds court to the north, its cup turned in welcome to the colder climes. The deep mysteries of the night office now fade with the promise of the sun.*

This is the time of dogs and roosters. The night creatures are returning to their dens, ready to report back to hungry children the success or failure of their labors. The dogs in the valley, invigorated after a night's rest, track the movements of each skunk, opossum, and fox that has crossed and still crosses their path. Agitated barking from all points of the compass signals a last hurdle for the weary parents trying to get home.

I sit in a chair I have brought for the occasion and let the sounds of this ending enter. The past few days I have hosted a cousin and his family. They were paying a visit to the last surviving sister of our mothers. As our aunt closes in on ninety-seven, she is still healthy and sharp. Yet her long day must inevitably near its close. Her offices observed with intelligence and faithfulness, she has achieved what our old dependable scribe Mr. Berry would term "a complete life."

One step in front of another and a life of daily cycles becomes a decade, a century, a millennium, a billion years. It's not for my intelligence to know the duration. And it's only for others to judge the completeness of my projects, to wonder what tasks I left unfinished, to know whether my footsteps traveled on a purposeful path or toward a dead-end. I resolve to be like the moon: Does she wonder if she should alter her footpath? No, she sets her course and sticks to it, knowing her place, her duties, a life faithful and true.

I gather my chair and head toward the house. The rooster crows now, answered from over the ridge. The light of the sun, still another hour below the eastern hill, respectfully waits for night to finish its work. My dogs disappear into the brush. The cool air moves, bringing the scent of a skunk disturbed by their explorations.

I leave them to patrol the farm, and I enter the house, first one foot and then the other.

For many years and on many occasions, both personally and professionally, I've given the offhand advice, "Hire the farm kid." Sometimes it has been meant as a literal instruction, but at least as often it has been given as a more general recommendation to hire the person who has a history of family work. It could be the woman who as a child cleared tables, placed orders, and ran the register every evening and weekend at her parent's restaurant, or the man who grew up cleaning boats at his father's marina. The advice either way remains the same: Look for the person who learned a work ethic early and applied it often. The person who in the formative years wasn't given the choice of whether to pull his or her weight is the one you want.

Many have been the paid youth and volunteers to have worked on this farm. The current Kid lives on a nearby farm and reports here every Saturday at 8:30 sharp. As part of our routine, I always ask him how his week has been, how his morning has been. The latter is something that isn't typically relevant except to the farm kid. On any given Saturday this Kid has already been out weeding in the family garden, feeding the livestock, helping his older brother load a hog for market, all before showing up here to work some more.

Countless are the tasks that make it onto the average farm's daily to-do list—a list, I should add, that isn't constrained by the hours in an eight-hour workday. Likewise, I ask as the Kid is leaving, what does he have on tap for the rest of the day? More often than not, his post-work chores include mowing the yard, cleaning the barn stalls, inspecting his bee colonies. . . .

The ethic of the farm-raised youth came to mind recently as I waited for the Kid to show up to work. Historically our children would have grown up in a farm community, and most of their peers would have had a similar work background. But today, when they are coddled at home well into and past adulthood, what is it like for our Kid to get on the school bus and find common ground? When his list of chores to complete morning and evening runs up against the latest video game or TikTok distraction of his peers, what goes through his mind?

So I ask him what his friends think of his farm life. At first he has little to say (not unusual: we are in the midst of tearing out overgrown brambles from a fence line). But after lunch, as we clean and put away our tools, he replies by relating a story from when he was much younger than his current age of fifteen:

"When I was eight a neighbor offered my dad half shares on his square bales if we'd pick them up in the field and store them in his barn. I couldn't pick them up [they can weigh fifty to seventy-five pounds], so I rolled them down the hill to my brothers. It took us all day. The neighbor had two sons who were sixteen and eighteen, and they never came out of the house to help. He said he couldn't ever get them to work. I thought that was odd. But I felt pretty good to be able to do something they couldn't."

Clearly, there is a difference between "a farm kid" and "a kid raised on a farm." And so my advice remains the same: "Hire the farm kid." And if you have the opportunity, raise a farm kid.

It is around six o'clock, and I have a full day ahead. I start as I do every day: grind the coffee, pour in the water, hit the on switch, pour the coffee down the gullet, and like magic the eyes open. The day's to-do list is long, too long, and I know full well that half the tasks will not get done. But I slip on my Wellingtons and tromp off through the wet grass to at least get the feeding and watering done early.

The sun is sleeping in, and what was a full moon is about to take a swan dive in the west. A replacement rooster is replying from the other side of the garden to his experienced counterpart in the coop. Like an artillery barrage they volley back and forth. The younger rooster sends the message, "I'm still here, old man." The old man has his reply ready, "Yeah, so who's sleeping in the weeds and who's sleeping with the ladies?"

Otherwise all is quiet until the rattle of the cans. Ginger, our workhorse, comes to the gate expectantly. I grab a small amount of feed and lead her out to her pasture. A bit more grain for the sheep and I call Becky, our English shepherd, to the corral. I position her to the left, just outside of the barn door. Opening it, I step back as the flood of sheep, like an unstoppable river current, bursts through the doorway.

Becky has little to do except act as the bouncer at this rowdy bar, serving as a reminder that bad behavior has consequences. She walks up on a few ewes who'd rather graze in the wrong pasture. They tuck tail and scurry to catch up with the others. Once the flock is safe in the proper field, I close the gate and leave them there for the day.

A bit of scratch and layer pellets goes to the chickens, then I open the door to the run and let them out. Most ignore the grains and head directly to the barnyard in search of grubs. The early bird, as they say.

The cattle graze quietly at the top of the pasture. I give them a handful of grain every few days, mainly so they know to come when called. As they drift en masse, they look like barges coursing slowly across a bay of grass, not a care in the world.

The pigs are packed in the freezers of six different families. Our new crop will arrive in another week. Chores done, I walk to the front of the barn and gaze down the hill, watching the fog rise from the creek bottom across the road. It moves, with a mind of its own, swiftly down the valley, clearly on a mission. I leave the view behind, feeling peaceful at the start of a busy day.

It's St. Patrick's Day, and our guests will begin arriving in the next hour for an annual dinner of corned pork cooked with cabbage and potatoes from the farm. The invited friends attend less out of any shared Irish heritage and more for the opportunity of a convivial evening of good food, drink, and conversation.

While our final preparations have moved forward, one of the young Katahdin ewes has been trying to lamb. She has been walking around in the pasture showing all the usual signs—pacing, standing up and lying down, pawing the ground. We've been checking frequently on the ewe's progress, and those signs now include a very large head protruding from her birth canal. We leave her alone for a while longer, hoping she will be able to lamb without assistance. Half an hour later, she has shown no more signs of progress, so we move her into a lambing pen in the barn.

It's five minutes before the guests are scheduled to arrive. We are both dressed for the get-together, not fancy duds, but nevertheless scrubbed and in fresh clothes. The ewe has made no further progress, so we decide it is time to intervene. Cindy washes up and, as I hold the laboring ewe, puts a hand in the birth canal and extracts the lamb's forelegs. The head is grotesquely swollen and shows no sign of life. Applying pressure in sync with the ewe's contractions, Cindy gradually pulls the lamb out. She then begins gently swinging it by all four legs and hands it off to me to continue the exercise.

I grasped the slippery legs and swing, with zero conviction that there is any life left in the limp body. Within seconds, however, I see the lamb begin to breathe. Cindy fills a water pail while I rub the newborn vigorously to stimulate blood flow. The lamb is a striking dark golden red, and it is huge, at least ten pounds. She looks exactly like a pint-size Hereford calf.

Satisfied with the outcome, we emerge from the barn, spattered with gore, to find our guests beginning to pull up in their cars and trucks. We welcome each arrival, then take them one by one into the barn to show off the mother and baby. The lamb, head-swelling reduced, is already on its feet nursing and seems no worse for the long afternoon of entering the world.

The vivid memory comes back in detail this week as I drive my truck to the slaughterhouse. That golden red lamb, now grown and with two lambings of her own, has reached the end of her time on our farm. Her Katahdin mother is a hair breed, but her father is a woolly red-faced Tunis. The cross has resulted in a ewe with a thick red wool coat. We have no interest in wool and no time or equipment to shear a wool coat. So this ewe and similar crosses are being culled from our breeding program.

It strikes me how odd this familiar scenario is: to be both the giver of life and the deliverer to the executioner. This large ewe is a beautiful creature, noble even, I note, as I watch her standing in the truck bed in the rearview mirror. I pull into Morgan's Meat Processing and turn the golden red ewe over to the care of the man who will kill and butcher her. After concluding my business in the front office, I pull back onto the highway. A last look in the mirror, then nothing remains but the memory and a new view ahead.

The wind has been up and blowing hard in the high crowns of the oaks since dawn. The crows seem to love these times, their caws to each other in the trees having only recently returned to the soundscape—a clear indication that fall is near. The crows radiate intelligence, black shrouds of solemnity observing the change of the season.

The maple leaves are turning backwards, a prelude to dying in a burst of color in another month or two. The woods are dense with an undergrowth of seedlings and brush. Rabbits seem to occupy the corner of every glance, as does the telltale flag of the deer bounding to just out of sight. The high today of seventy-two is welcome after the recent late summer blast of ninety degrees.

A few evenings ago Cindy and I were both involved in the type of farming accident that is always lurking in the background. An inexperienced draft horse panicked and bolted as we hooked her to a work sled. Cindy jumped from the runaway sled, and both of us got tangled in one of the fences the horse took down in her effort to escape the perceived predator at her heels. We emerged cut, bloodied, bruised, battered, and clothes in tatters. Fortunately neither of us ended up in the hospital, or worse, but we acknowledged that things certainly could have gone either way. The cawing of the crows to each other overhead as we made our way back into the house relayed the news the old-fashioned way.

The next morning I caught a flight to my homeland of Southwest Louisiana. It's a place where the honorific "Mr." or "Miss" still precedes the first name of an elder when addressed by someone younger. Walking about town with my dad, then eighty-seven, I watched with admiration as he was greeted repeatedly with a friendly "Hello, Mr. Bill." At a farmer's market children approached my sister Kathryn with a respectful "Miss Kat."

At a fast-food restaurant I was pleasantly surprised to find that the same salutation was used with customers: a call for "Mr. Brian" and I was handed my breakfast.

No crows heralded my arrival at or departure from my ancestral home. But no announcement was needed to convey the shades of change coming in the not-too-distant future. Life is, as they say, terminal, and unlike the ancient Romans we do not need to consult the entrails of a slaughtered bullock to recognize the inevitable cycles of life. With my family in the evening, in a house filled with laughter, I observed my father, surrounded by his children, grandchildren, and great-grandchildren. The next morning, he was still hale and hearty as we two stood in the graveyard. The tombstones of my mother, sister, and brother as well as my own father's mother, aunt, and father stood in front of us. Without sadness my father pointed out where he and my stepmother would be buried when their time came.

Farming as we do fine tunes an appreciation of the cycles of life: listening for the peep of newly emerging chicks and butchering a rooster, savoring the first juicy tomato of summer and the last winter squash of fall, welcoming a squirming new pup and helping an old dog as she struggles to rise from stiff slumber, grieving the death of a sister and sharing a glass of wine with her daughter.

The seasons change, the wheel turns, and the crows always come back.

Beyond the brilliant red on the maple outside my study, the shots of hunters at both daybreak and sundown indicate that fall has well and truly arrived.

Saturday morning is spent in the usual pursuit of running errands and clearing the slate of farm chores and tasks. I do not achieve full success in either. Afternoon finds me bushhogging a twelve-acre pasture. A soothing act, the cut grass revealing the smooth curve of the landscape, it is also a meditative one, one that allows time for the mind to float along unexpected paths. As I finish in the early evening, the crack of firearms in the distance pulls me back from any reverie. The cattle look up, mutter something the rough equivalent of "Humans!" and go back to grazing.

I enter the house for our evening coffee to find that Cindy has baked a platter of homemade shortbread cookies. For some reason this has me thinking about the pursuit of what in our global consumer culture have been dismissed as the "archaic arts." These are arts not clearly connected with the culture of global commerce—which is not to say that they are not connected with commerce, of course.

I have spent my adult life in the mines of the book industry, an art-form-turned-business-model locked in classic overshoot, where the issuance of new works has not yet registered the collapse of readership, where the vein we have followed of new readers has petered and faltered and is near to playing out, where an intelligent youth of a nearby farm, eighteen years of age, told me recently, without embarrassment, that he has never read a book by choice.

During a short visit with a sister in Arkansas this week I found her pursuing a similar arc as my own, in her case teaching classical European ballet. She has run a vibrant and popular dance academy for many years, yet she faces the difficulty of capturing an audience for an art form that doesn't come with tweets and likes. She has the dedicated dancers of the discipline. But in our 24/7 world of digital and visual distractions, where is the audience that can discern a plié from an arabesque, or that cares that there is a difference?

Global culture is a consumer culture. Its goal is growth on a finite planet, a car for everyone in China and India, farmed shrimp from Indonesia on every Iowa farmer's plate. It is fundamentally a disposable culture.

Disposable products, people, and planet. It has little use for the arts of an enduring culture. The dance that requires long study, the book written a hundred years ago, the technique of preserving soil fertility organically—all are archaic: they don't require a container ship to deliver them to our doors.

There are still niches for the archaic arts. And it is our job to help preserve them, to help them endure through the cacophony and clutter of the modern world. While the era of mass literacy and the literature it spawned may be coming to an end, it doesn't mean that literacy and the written word are also going to be lost. Audiences for disciplined and focused dance may be in retreat, but the participants are still queuing up to learn.

We on a small farm are learning the archaic arts—harvesting manure to build soil fertility, constructing secure fences that do indeed make good neighbors, planting vegetables that when they mature will feed us for a month or more, creating a plate of shortbread cookies that nourishes the soul—and all connect us with long-passed practitioners of these arts in ways that Facebook and Walmart never can and never will. These are the arts that make us more fully a community, a culture, a people.

The sounds of farm life are, overall, pleasing, conducive to a reflective life. A quiet morning walk to complete chores before sunup, the soft thud of chickens jumping off the roost to greet me; a mid-afternoon amble through the woods, a light drizzle muting the outside world; even the reassuring rumble of my elderly neighbor's tractor across the ridge—all help quiet the rumpus of this modern life.

Morning chore time is my chance to evaluate what needs to be done for the day. As I feed, water, and move the animals to their daily pastures I am mentally recording my to-do list: finish installing the new electric fence line, clean out and refill the sheep watering trough, add fresh bedding to the chicken coop, reattach the gutter to the barn. It's a constantly evolving list, one I need only remember until I'm in the house and can record it on paper.

But as the fall changes into winter, so do the livestock's expectations and so too does my opportunity for introspection. When fresh grass gets scarce and the animals transition to hay, the cattle and sheep become more vocal. They will eat the hay, but they miss the grass. So for the first hour in the morning, at this time of the year, the ewes run around bleating, loudly. The cattle catch sight of me and thunder down the hill, bawling all the way.

My ability to form and retain my to-do list in these times unravels further with each bleat and bawl. Finish installing new electr . . . baahh. Let's see, clean out and refill . . . something . . . baahhh, baahhh, baaaahhhhh. Reattach . . . baaaaaaaahhhhhhhhhhhh. I feel like the Vonnegut character living in a dystopian world where the IQs are leveled by subjecting the brighter individuals to periodic earsplitting noises. Perhaps the sheep have conspired to . . . baaaaaaaaaaaahhhhhhhhhhhh. Now, what was I starting to do?

It is both a joy and a curse to have a tin roof on the farmhouse. The joy is in hearing when the slightest patter of rain moves in, an experience that is easily missed on the now-conventional shingles. No need to tune in to the electronic device for the forecast, much less peer out the window, to know which way the wind blows.

The curse is that that same roof serves as an unwanted alarm clock, whether in the middle of the night or in the predawn hours. It's a wake-up call that the barn jacket is still hanging on the fence post, that a favorite hand tool is in the back of the pickup, that you have a dozen tasks to complete outside, rain or shine. Once awake, you hear the dogs bark . . . and you start wondering if Delores has escaped her paddock again. And so the day begins. Your brain shifts into gear, and you roll out of bed, reluctantly, and get dressed. And as you make coffee and step out into the early morning, whatever rain you may have heard on that tin roof has moved on to other pastures. The day, when it dawns, will be with clear skies.

As I go about my chores on this morning I find that no new lambs have been born and the new hog, Delores, is still contained. Morning rounds the day before had revealed a ewe with brand new healthy twins. As with all births, mother and newborns were separated into a lambing pen, where they would be kept for a day or two. The maternity ward gives us a chance to observe and a chance for the new mom to adequately bond with her offspring. Once the lambs have begun nursing and the ewe recognizes their smell, the family is turned out with the other new mothers and their charges.

We spent the bulk of the morning reinforcing one of the pig paddocks near the gardens in preparation for receiving an incoming pregnant gilt. We had not intended to get back into maintaining breeding stock, but a number of our local sources for feeder pigs had troubles this winter that left them with nothing to show for their labors. That, rightfully, should be a warning to us as well. But we plunged ahead and made a bargain to purchase Delores instead. She should farrow for the first time around the beginning of March.

Delores, an all-black yearling of about 200 pounds, had of recent been a pet. The woman selling her had not realized just how fast and large pigs grow. Cindy left late morning to pick up the hog about twenty-five miles south. Meanwhile, I spent the time butchering and cleaning roosters.

I am just finishing scrubbing down the equipment after packaging and freezing the birds when Cindy returns, pig in tow. We have a quick late lunch, then easily introduce Delores into her new, spacious digs. We secure her with the final bit of fencing, give her fresh water, and retire for an afternoon nap.

Awaking refreshed, we share coffee before heading out to do our late afternoon chores. Dinner guests are set to arrive within a couple of hours, and we still need to prepare the food. We stop by the pig paddock first. Spotting the hog panel thrown up at an odd angle, we know immediately that we are minus one 200-pound gilt.

Delores, in the space of an hour and half, has escaped from her paddock through an unsecured panel, trundled down a ravine, been discovered in a neighbor's front yard and enticed into a goat pen, escaped from that pen, and walked back up the hill into the ravine. And that is where we find her, 200 yards down a steep overgrown hill from where she had begun to explore the countryside. It should have ended in catastrophe. But within five minutes Delores has followed Cindy, and a bucket of feed, back home. We spend the next thirty minutes reinforcing the fencing, then completing chores, before returning to the house to cook for our evening guests.

Which is undoubtedly why, this morning at four o'clock, I awoke to the feather-light rain on the metal roof and wondered, "Where is Delores?"

After securing the sheep for the night, I step out of the front door of the barn to survey our modest holdings. A couple of cold weeks and heavy rains have left a slurry of frozen mud and muck at the entrance. The few bales of straw we've laid down to soak up the mess did help . . . temporarily, but in the long term they have only made it worse. For straw now serves as a deceptive floating raft on the mire. It's a perch that I quickly realize will not long support my 200-pound body—a body that, once launched, slips the surly bonds for a brief moment before gravity pulls it back to earth, ending its uninspiring descent in a long slide, with only a hay bale intervening to slow its progress.

Odd how dignity attempts to reinstate itself in the most unlikely of situations. There I am, one moment wallowing in the mire, a solid streak of mud caked on one side from ear to calf, yet mere seconds later bounding up out of the muck as if nothing has happened, all for the benefit of the watching sheep and pigs.

Well, there is nothing dignified about a grown man stripping down to his birthday suit on the front porch, temperature thirty-four degrees, before being allowed entry to his own home. But thanks to a capacious hot water tank, I do reemerge with an acceptable standard of hygiene and a new appreciation of terra firma.

We do try. But I won't declare that we do the best job of caring for our land. You see, I know where the bodies are buried: the troublesome spots of erosion, the areas of overuse, diseased trees, and neglected infrastructure. Yet I won't underestimate our hard work and successes at stewarding this farm of seventy acres. That stewardship will, we hope, leave the land upon our departure in better shape than when we took up this way of life.

Nonetheless, we are both aware of the potential futility of these efforts in a world overburdened by population, climate change, resource depletion, and the general collapse of good behavior. Even as I type these words I can view the neighboring hills, a mile in distance, denuded of trees from a poorly executed clear-cut, a process that is repeated up and down our small valley.

At times our farm seems an island in a sea of abuse. Small farms are no more immune to poor practices than large farms. Perhaps the small farm has a bit more flexibility; it is closer to the root of a problem and so can respond in real time. Like an aluminum V-hull compared to an ocean liner, it is more maneuverable. But it is no nobler for its small size. I seem to recall that Orwell, in his book *The Road to Wigan Pier*, makes a reference to small landlords being worse than large ones because of their limited resources to improve their investments. Similarly, the small farm is just as subject to market forces and has the same drive to wring every bit of profit from the fewer resources at hand as its larger counterpart. It's a sad play that has us repeating our role in the original sin: we are shorting tomorrow for a bite of an apple today.

This all leaves me, as I look out my window, thinking that this island that is our farm is already being lapped by the rising waters of our future. Yet we continue to make our efforts to stake a claim to an imaginable future that has room for well-cared-for small farms, families, and communities on a healthy planet. To that end we gathered last night with other area small farmers for an evening of fellowship, food, and conversation. To that end our sow, Delores, farrowed in the early hours of this morning. And to that end we plant today a new vineyard of wine grapes. That is the present and future as best as we can manage, for now.

Winter is beginning to lose its grip. The signs are there if you are not moving too fast to see or hear.

After a Friday morning low of sixteen degrees, Saturday afternoon saw the temperature pass sixty. The elderberry bushes have new leaves, while the hazelnuts are sending up fresh suckers. Bird life of all sorts, both wild and domestic, has returned to the soundscape. At the nearby farm of friends, wood frogs serenade the evening with throaty mating calls down by the creek.

The bins of seed potatoes have all sprouted and await the day when the gardener finds sufficient energy to plant. As the days lengthen, egg production of our twenty hens has grown from nil to an even half-dozen a day. Another couple of weeks and we'll be gathering a dozen a day. One more week and our Speckled Sussex hens will go broody. Three weeks after that the chicks will be tumbling out of every nook and cranny of the barn.

The pasture grass is still brown from a distance. But get in close and you'll see the green shoots beginning to peek through. The trees appear barren from afar, but approach them and a different story can be read— tight buds on the plums, peaches, and maples. The land is waking back up. Having replenished its energy and reformulated its plans, it is ready to give it a go for another year.

Even people are venturing out in minor numbers. On a drive about town we spot the elusive modern teenager tossing hoops with a friend. We pass on the temptation to slow and observe their behavior; such rare activity of the species should not be interfered with.

Rounding a corner we see a man polishing his bass boat. Since when did fishing boats become toys? When did a simple jon boat with some sturdy tackle, ample lures, and a trotline to check at night become not good enough? Since when have we needed depth finders and a boat that costs more than a modest home? When was the quiet joy of casting for bass or bream on a still pond replaced by the sounds of the Bristol Speedway on our waters? Jon boat vs. bass boat —perhaps that is the tale of our age and our race: a slow pace propelled by paddles or a hurried dashing to and fro.

This spring I've made some resolutions: To walk and not run through the season. To get down close, with my hands in the dirt, and feel the change. To sit more on the porch with family and friends and say nothing, listening instead to the frogs by the pond or for the sound of the moon rising. To walk among the sheep at night. Stand among the fruit trees and just look. Put a plump worm on a hook, toss it into a likely sheltered spot, and just wait.

It's time to wake back up and see if we are worthy to give it a go for another year.

The initial thrill that comes with an ice storm and a loss of power fades a bit the morning the temperature bottoms out at three degrees. Delores the sow has dragged the heater out of her water trough for the fifth time, the pond ice for the cattle and horse has to be broken every few hours, and a young ewe and her newborn have to be rescued after lambing in a far corner of the wind-blown sheep pasture and relocated to the shelter of a barn stall. Still, the domestic pleasure of coming into a cozy house heated by a woodstove to sip a hot cup of tea provides a large measure of compensation.

Traditionally we built our houses to meet the demands of our climates, a grass hut if you lived on a tropical isle and a house with connected barn if you lived in New England. Older houses in Louisiana, when I was growing up, were typically built a couple of feet off the ground. It was a good model for a warm climate. The open space underneath kept the house cooler in the warmer months (most of the year), and the elevation protected against the occasional flooding. Freezes, like the big one in 1940 that my father recalled, were rare. And given that most plumbing in that earlier time was limited to the kitchen, freeze damage to the house was minimal.

Infrastructure was on my mind this past week here in East Tennessee. After a week of temperatures barely budging above freezing, the ice storm hit, the power failed, and the temperature plummeted. Thankfully, we have a generator to run the refrigerator and freezers and a few essential electrical circuits. We have a manual well pump that can override the electric one, and a Jøtul woodstove keeps the house a comfortable sixty degrees. Another generator at the barn supports the plug-in heaters in the various watering troughs, providing ice-free drinking water for the livestock.

The electricity that keeps the modern house functioning is a relatively new concept in human culture, having only taken off in the late nineteenth century. But since that time the line between what is and isn't "essential" has shifted seismically. Today our houses are designed to accommodate the necessities that just a generation ago were not needed, nor even available. Shelter, heat, food, and water now share demand with internet, smartphone, cable TV, and microwave.

Older forms of infrastructure had built-in resilience: barns carefully constructed to hold heat, with hay mows above to ease the feeding of livestock in poor weather; deep in-ground cisterns to provide fresh water for the farm; houses designed to facilitate warmth in the winter and coolness in the summer. All are smart low-tech designs that we have pushed aside with the assumption that the power grid will now take care of us.

Over the years Cindy and I have discussed converting our farm to an off-the-grid power system. Each time, though, we found the costs to be prohibitive. But this week, after a few days without power, as we scrambled to keep up with ours and our livestock's basic needs, it occurred to me: Off-the-grid is easy. It is our needs today that are complicated, the prohibitive factor, the stumbling block, the real expense.

The old houses of South Louisiana worked year in, year out, because they had very little modern infrastructure to protect. Working in the crawl space to insulate each individual pipe before the ice storm, I was overwhelmed by how much plumbing is needed in our small house just to furnish us with water on demand. Hot and cold pipes to the kitchen and two bathrooms, the hot water heater and the washer/dryer—a complexity of plumbing requiring protection from the elements, so that it might protect us from the elements.

Driving into town late in the week I see dozens of downed trees, limbs still balancing on utility lines, brush pushed to the edges of the road. As I look at the miles of power and telephone lines, our true vulnerability is evident. It is not only the loss of electrical power that we fear but the loss of a certain status that comes with modern life, a status of predictability.

Off-the-grid literature is typically geared toward finding ways around the commercial power source while still retaining the modern conveniences. As we water and feed our sheep, as lambs are born this week without regard to the temperature or the state of our utilities, I think about the Amish. While many of us were without power, were they concerned with their inability to update their Facebook pages, charge their cell phones, keep their freezers going, stay warm with their electric furnaces? Did they feel powerless? Somehow I doubt it.

The complexity of this modern life, the infrastructure that maintains it, is hardwired for disruption. Our system and our expectations for what it must provide are such that losing power is a form of powerlessness. To me that seems a form of slavery, which is why I always experience that bit of anarchic joy in an emergency, an unshackling from the system, though, as I'll also admit, that uncertain joy is accompanied by relief when the master comes home and power is restored.

No sooner has the young vet climbed out of the cattle chute than our two farm dogs, Becky and Teddy, dart away, both with a bull testicle dangling from their mouths. It's a macabre sight but one all too familiar to anyone spending time on a farm.

As I write out a check, our vet stretches his shoulder to work out a kink where a 500-pound young bull has kicked him. *All in a day's work,* I think. The rain is pouring down on the last day of winter, the barnyard is ankle deep in muck, yet the farm vet emerges with a grin on his face. No doubt he has chosen the right profession. I recall last year, when on a snowy January day he cheerfully came out one Sunday morning and put a prolapsed uterus back in a favored ewe.

His predecessor, before he retired, had sported the same demeanor: always cheerful, whether working in rain or sun. On a similar day to this, but years back, the elder vet was castrating a long line of recently purchased weanling bull calves. He jumped into the chute, exclaiming, "Let the rodeo begin!" Whereupon he was promptly stomped and kicked for his enthusiasm.

These are curious days in the large-animal vet field. Nationally, 80 percent of all graduates from vet school are women. Women can certainly do large-animal work, but most choose not to. Being a farm vet isn't as high-paying as being a small-animal or equine vet, and the few who pursue a large-animal career choose the more lucrative equine field. As poet-vet Baxter Black says, the anthropomorphological attachment that exists in the pet world does not extend to livestock: why spend $100 on a ewe that may only bring $110 at the stockyard?

Traditionally most large-animal vets were men who came from a farming background. As the number of family farms and farm families plummeted, so too did the number of young males who valued that life. Valuing the farm life seems an essential to anyone, man or woman, who contemplates such a robust career as a large-animal vet. Combining a love for the physical demands of the farm vet with the educational drive and academic ability to get in and through vet school reduces the number of prospects even further.

The dearth of farm vets, coupled with economics, means that those of us who farm livestock learn to do much of the doctoring ourselves, and Cindy and I do carry out most of the castrating, worming, vaccinating, assisting with births, and other nonsurgical doctoring. Still, not having trained professionals available for that prolapsed uterus, for that cow that ingests a nail, or for any of the other seemingly infinite number of ways in which an animal's health can be imperiled is worrisome.

Watching our youthful vet jump back in his truck, wave, and drive off to his next round, I'm relieved that in spite of the shortage of farm vets across rural America, our needs appear to be met for some time to come.

A midnight thunderstorm sounds its prelude an hour before arrival . . . with a soft thud of feet on our front door as Becky, our English shepherd stock-dog, signals that she has heard the distant rumbling and wants to come inside. I walk downstairs and put her on the back porch and return to bed.

After the storm has moved through, a steadier wind comes rattling down our small valley to shake the windows. A cold front has arrived, and most of the night will pass before it manages to crowd out the warmth of the previous day.

At three in the morning the familiar refrain of short, high-pitched yapping informs me that our other dogs are onto the scent of a small varmint. The barking follows its target, nose to ground, on a rapid serpentine trail, first near the barn, then through the orchard, and finally, dear God, just beyond the bedroom window. Apparently taken by surprise, the quarry resorts to its most effective defense. The acrid smell of the skunk will linger until long after sunrise.

I return to my sleep until around five, when the rhythms of morning begin to edge out those of the night. A rooster reminds me that we forgot to close the chicken run gate last evening. He uses his improvised perch in the grapevines to challenge a sun that won't arrive for another couple of hours.

My brain shifts unbidden into wakefulness. In squawky images it starts to review the tasks of the day ahead: moving piglets to a new paddock away from the sow, shifting electric fence for the cattle to a new stretch of spring grass, cleaning the gutters on the house and outbuildings, collecting for compost winter's leftovers from the hay rings in the pastures. I rise and make coffee as the night disappears into the west.

Looking down at a long row of spiny pigweed intercropped with my crowder peas, I feel a minor cousin of weltschmerz washing over me. Seemingly sprung to life overnight, the pigweed's thorny presence towers above the peas planted six weeks ago, offering a clear indictment of my abilities, perhaps even my character.

But what is this I'm feeling? What form of cowardice is this to shrink back from the world because a weed persists in an unwelcome spot? Did my species rise up out of the dust of the Cretaceous only to have one of its members recoil from such an innocuous foe? Will I so easily accept defeat? Apparently, yes. . . . I throw down my gardener's implements, grab a beer, and retreat to the hammock. Perhaps after the next extinction event runs its course the spiny amaranth will develop consciousness and proceed to do better than we have with this poor planet.

Battling prickly foe has not been the first challenge of the day. Earlier, I tried to caponize a cockerel for the first time. It's a procedure that entails cutting between the second and third rib of a young bird, extracting the male internal reproductive gland, then allowing the skin to snap back into place and seal the incision.

With my caponizing kit laid neatly on the table—rib spreaders, probe, scalpel—I begin by strapping the cockerel down with cord. Gripping the how-to pamphlet in my left hand, I pick the pin feathers away with my right. Instructed by the pamphlet to follow the hip bone and find the ribs, I swab the designated section with rubbing alcohol and probe with my index finger, counting: one rib, two ribs. Rib spreaders standing by, I grab the scalpel and make ready to incise.

But where did the ribs go? They seemed so clearly in evidence only a second before. The scalpel hangs like Damocles' sword over the little bird. "Make the cut anyway; you'll figure it out," I tell myself. I hover, the bird passively awaiting his fate, and start to sweat.

Seconds later I find myself loosening the cord. I pick up the cockerel and release him, unscathed, into the population of would-be gumbos and coqs au vin blithely scratching about the farm. The capon of a future feast will come at the hands of a different surgeon, one of courage and surer anatomical knowledge.

That failure is what drives me to the garden, certain at least of my competence in that department. The eyes of 10,000 years of agriculture follow my movements with intimate nods of confidence, whereupon, seeing the unruly and unwelcome pigweed, I flee.

Ah, for the simple joy of the hammock. This I can do.

The South is a Neolithic fort.

It is in a Steak 'n Shake in Georgia, standing in a swirl of moderns with their faux tribal tattoos and piercings, that a small girl protectively holds the weathered fingers of her grandfather. He stands erect in his worn overalls, both hands slightly curled, as if gripping the wooden handles of a plow, looking out of place.

Observing him, it strikes me that all of the people, the building, and the parking lot are intruders and interlopers, a mirage: the old man is standing in the same pose, in the same place in a tobacco plot, hands wrapped just so around the plow handles, two mules out front and a granddaughter by his side.

The South is like this. Sometimes it is a Neolithic fort in the landscape, a slight rise in the ground indicating the presence of a past for those who can read it, a place full of relics and behaviors that are deemed out of place in a culture easily bored and distracted. It is not a landscape effortlessly read by the digital world or understood by soundbite.

It has a people, black and white, who are looked down on and discarded because they have not adapted quickly enough, modest people who don't know that a paved parking lot has more value than a small field of their own. It has an agrarian soul and a heart that still beats.

This South is a run-down home, chickens scratching around the yard. Its roosters crow at all hours, riling the neighbor from up north who built a McMansion next door, an outsider who did not know pigs can stink. It is a make-do world where fences get built out of scaffolding discarded by a now defunct warehouse, a world often stubbornly ignorant of the rewards of 9–5 and cultures bought and traded on Netflix.

It is a world that doesn't easily discard anything, even the burdens of the past, a world easily mocked with sitcom humor by a world in which advanced degrees in identity politics measure a culture to the failed standard of a "New Man" emerging.

Drive down the backroads of our valley and find gatherings of men sitting on shaded porches in the midday heat. Surrounded by well-tended gardens, with chickens scratching and kids in the dirt, they talk sedition and plot the downfall of the moderns using an elaborate plan called Waiting Them Out. Meanwhile, they buy nothing new, grow their own food, slaughter their own chickens, hunt their own game, and grip the handles of the plow.

Join them if you wish . . . or not. They don't care.

3

Prime

JUST AFTER SUNRISE IS *an active office, a time for movement and chores, a time when reflection and observation are often drunk on the go, when dark gives way to light and to shadows. This begins the dutiful time of day, when the role of husbanding demands an attentive service. It is a time of rivers.*

The back door shuts, a signal carried to the barnyard and picked up by the slumbering ram. He rises, and the bell around his neck wakens the flock. The ewes rise in unison. They gather together with expectant murmuring, awaiting my arrival. An open gate, a shaken bucket of feed, and the river rushes forward, eddies around my legs, erodes my stability before flooding into the fresh grass: a flock experiencing the full pleasure of an early spring morning. The chickens mirror in lesser volume the actions of their ovine sisters. They stream out of the coop and into the sunlight, bugs and scratch high on their list of priorities.

Below the farm, down the hill at the road, the world of man has begun to reassert a misshapen dominance. The two-lane highway, a rising water approaching flood stage, threatening to overwhelm, is quickly engorged by the tributaries of commuter cars and trucks flowing into its main channel. Among them, a school bus moves in and out of the road current, accumulating children, eventually depositing them like a debris field after a storm, to be trained in the finer points of boredom and disengagement.

After an hour or two the morning flood will subside to a trickle before the mystery reverses itself in late afternoon. In the meantime my path is a well-trodden one of scheduled rituals, starting with feeding and watering all who need it. I end the office leaning over the paddock fence. I watch with pleasure as the pigs enjoy (in a way that only pigs can) their early morning breakfast—a pause in my activities, a quiet few minutes to review the day to come.

I turn from those in my care now fed, the initial flow of morning chores observed, and return to the house for my own breakfast. The fine blue sky is now streaked with half a dozen contrails, sad evidence of our misplaced search for wonderment.

When death arrives in the country, the signs go up at the roadside: "Slow, Death in Family" on the front, funeral home name on the back, in case passersby want to send flowers or attend the funeral or have an ailing relative who might soon need services of his own.

Sometimes we know a neighbor has passed away because we see the unknown vehicles parked in the yard and the unknown clan members congregated on the porch, dressed in their Sunday best. Or the phone rings and a neighbor who seldom calls informs us that another neighbor has died. Or there's an obituary in the local paper. Or a new mound of dirt appears at the Cedar Fork Baptist Church cemetery.

This culture likes to think it's more connected, "wired" in to the world. The reality is that the technology of the day distances us from what matters. That separation has been coming for a century or more, as village life and the interconnectedness of communities have unraveled.

It's a process accelerated by the arrival of the automobile. A highly impersonal mode of transportation, cheap motorized travel allowed us to drive away from our community obligations and connections. And now the digital world is putting an end to the daily arrival of the community newspaper, a medium in which people could keep up with the high school football scores, learn who was arrested for drunk driving, read the tedious notes from the county commission, and find out who died.

Our subscription to the local paper lapsed many years ago. Of course, we could still go online to read. That ritual, however, is not the same as sitting down and digesting the local paper over coffee. And for many complex reasons our new online rituals seldom inform as to the kith part of "kith and kin." We instead are more current on the latest fake news and fake outrage on Facebook.

With the collapse of face-to-face community and the readership of the local paper, so too collapses our knowledge of the people sharing our immediate world. Sometimes the "Slow, Death in Family" signs don't go up, and we discover a loss weeks or months later, leaving the deceased's family to wonder why no one offered condolences.

An accident a mile away from our home this week brought home that tragic point. Two cars collided. Three people were airlifted to a hospital and one to the morgue. While speaking with one neighbor about the tragedy, Cindy heard of the sudden passing of another neighbor's daughter a month ago. No signs, no gathering of cars, no call, and no dirt in the local cemetery alerted us, so the neighbor who lives directly across from our farm was allowed to grieve while thinking us callous or indifferent. True, we were not close with this particular neighbor, but that would not preclude the courtesy of our offering a sympathetic word.

Odd that as the world gets smaller our neighbors get further away.

I lay out my shotguns and deer rifle on a folding table outside the kitchen window. With fall around the corner, it is time to clean and oil the guns. It's a methodical process that is satisfying to undertake on objects that are a beautiful marriage of design and utility. Using a kit made for the purpose, I ram the cleaning rods through the barrels, oil the working parts, and rub the wood stocks till they shine. I finish just as guests arrive for dinner, and I return the guns to the cabinet as the visitors walk up the drive.

Growing up in Louisiana I hunted and fished year-round alongside my father and brother. It was a rare week that did not find me crouching in a duck blind, running trotlines, crabbing, or catching crawfish. Game, freshwater and saltwater fish, shrimp, and oysters easily provided five dinner meals out of seven for our household. Staying up late at night cleaning and gutting fish, setting the alarm every two hours to check the trotlines, waking up at three o'clock to get to the duck blind or be on the open gulf by sunrise—all were part of the landscape of my childhood.

Mine was the hunting and fishing of providence, not of the trophy hunter. It was the experience of a profoundly masculine world. From the catching, shooting, and cleaning to, in many cases, the cooking, it was a culture of men putting food on the table for their families. It wasn't needed in the middle-class home of my father—he certainly could have provided all of our meat needs from the grocery store—but it was a lifestyle I shared with most of my friends growing up.

There was always an exhilaration in making a good shot or setting a hook. It provided and still provides a sense of accomplishment that is part evolutionary and large part tribal. The camaraderie of men in camp, the solitude of the hunt, the contentment of being on the water by myself or with my father, the rituals of killing and of eating, each shaped who I am as a person.

Perhaps it is counterintuitive, but killing another living creature can teach a person a lot about nature. Putting that act of killing in its "proper place" reminds us of where we came from and where we belong. And remembering our place in a natural order may be the best way to save this planet.

A detractor could argue against the killing, the male role in that culture, and I would listen and perhaps agree in part. But my defense is simple and straightforward. I prefer to be the one with blood on his hands. I believe it is a stance that makes me more, not less, sensitive to the value of life. It is the same reason I butcher the farm's livestock. Doing so seems more honest.

As we collectively pile into our cars, while away our hours shopping, allow our kids to grow up without seeing the light of day as they game their way into perpetual adolescence, move from air-conditioned office to air-conditioned vehicle to air-conditioned home, with all that those actions entail for the planet, we might ask ourselves a hard question: who are we kidding? Whether we are vegetarians or meat eaters, just because we do not pull the trigger or set the hook does not mean we are not all culpable in the killing that our lives require.

There is a day each year, a day when you find yourself in the kitchen slicing the last of the season's ripe tomatoes, a moment you have lived before and have known was in the cards, a day when the vines are still heavy with green tomatoes, a shortened day in which those green tomatoes will never fully ripen, destined instead for frying or making chowchow. How did that unstoppable summer deluge become a trickle and then a drought?

So begins fall, a final chance to cherish what is passing before the weather turns to ice and snow—too soon for us to dream of the fallow winter, when the cold months spoon next to the season of rebirth, that bare season, stark in its absence of greenery, when our native imagination colors in the palette of the riches to come, and too late to partake of the plethora of fresh bounty of the summer season just passed. The in-between season.

Fall is the season of salvage, of scouring the fields and paddocks for useful leftovers. It's a time of rushing to harvest the last of the fruit to preserve in jams, jellies, chutneys, and wines. It is a time of movement, cattle to new pastures and forage to cover; of gleaning the excess hens and roosters and butchering for hours to stock the larder for the gumbo and chicken and dumplings that will get us through the cold months to come. It is a time to take stock with some soul-searching of Aesop's Fables significance: Do we have enough firewood? Did we use our time well last winter, spring, summer in preparation for the next year?

Fall is a time for hog fattening. The cruel reward for an ability to gain 300 pounds in nine months comes in the form of a knife wielded the week after Halloween. The bounty is delivered to us in sides of bacon, salted hams, corned shoulders, butcher's wife pork chops, hand-seasoned breakfast sausages, headcheese, pâté, and bowls of beans with ham hocks.

Fall is also sheep breeding time. As the days and nights cool, the ram has his pleasurable work cut out for him, making sure all ewes are bred. We, servant-like, make sure the ewes are conditioned for lambing, in good health, hooves trimmed, their every need attended to. Meanwhile, last winter's lambs graze in their own pasture, fattening before they too fall under the butcher's sword in the remaining months of the year.

Fall is the season of coming face to face with imminent and unavoidable death. It is the fever of the dying year, the mumbled words from the patient in the bed trying to get his affairs in order, to make amends. So much to do and so little time.

It is a season of contrasts, when we eat a ripe tomato while composting the vine it grew on, feed a pregnant ewe while fattening for slaughter her teenage offspring, crush grapes and pears while sipping the wine made last year. Past, present, and future are jumbled in this most hopeful season, when we weigh the year to come to see what is left in the balance. Like a culture that prepares for a future generation, we undertake this work for a year not yet born.

Bushhogging the hill pasture in preparation for winter, I come across again the large buck with the impressive antler spread. He leaps in front of the tractor, then bounds over a fence into a neighbor's field, which unbeknownst to the buck is a no-kill farm, a safe zone where he could, if he'd only stay put, live out his entire life without danger. I watch him run across the neighbor's field and jump another fence, and he is gone. Another circuit around the hill and I see a couple of trucks pull up at our farm. I head down and greet the youthful crew that has arrived to cut down four massive trees alongside our gravel driveway.

The trees, one white and three red oaks, need to be felled expertly to avoid nearby power lines and a neighbor's house. The men have to climb sixty feet and, from an eagle's perch, drop the limbs. Once the upper limbs are cut, the workers lay the trunks across the drive and cut them into ten-foot-long sawlogs. Ultimately, the largest logs are to be milled into lumber, the crowns mulched, the limbs cut into firewood, the stumps drilled and plugged with oyster mushroom spawn.

To dance high above the ground with running chainsaws is dangerous work, but it is done today with real purpose, joy, and competence, something that seems at odds with the lethargy of many young men I encounter. It's a lethargy that seems endemic: man-boys extending their adolescence well into adulthood, living at home, gliding into their thirties without experiencing responsibility.

Not so long ago 80 percent of American high schools offered vocational training. But in just a twenty-year span that percentage was reversed, including at our own rural school. Now boys (and girls as well) enter biological adulthood without getting any practical schooling in crafts that formerly allowed them to earn a living and, more important, self-respect. The fallout from this lack of preparation for honorable and satisfying work: a population of untrained and rudderless young men exemplified by an acquaintance of mine who drives forty miles to Knoxville to work in a call center selling jewelry to elderly women.

For reasons not fully understood, we continue to entertain the idea that all youth are destined for college. Without any statistical evidence, I'd still hazard a guess that the average electrician, plumber, or surveyor out-earns a significant portion of college grads.

My gut feeling that self-worth comes from tangible outcomes, whether raising livestock, felling trees, or wiring a barn, is backed up by personal experience—my own father's landscape, for example, where a lifetime as a construction engineer allowed him to see daily the evidence of an industrious life.

Matthew Crawford echoes this sentiment in his insightful book *Shop Class as Soulcraft*: "The satisfaction of manifesting oneself concretely in the world through manual competence has been known to make a man quiet and easy. He can simply point: the building stands, the car now runs, the lights are on. Boasting is what a boy does, because he has no real effect on the world."

Should the young men fed into our current system, one that devalues particular competence and focused physical activity, descend into a lifetime of malaise and meaningless boasting, it will not come as a surprise. Nor will it be any surprise should those rural young men who find employment in crafts, trades, or farming have a stronger sense of purpose and self-worth.

As the day ends on the farm, the men of the cutting crew get in their pickups. They grin, wave, and drive away: another job well done but without ceremony.

One hundred and eighty-some years ago, while Andrew Jackson was president, around the year the Cherokee signed the treaty to vacate these lands, a white oak seedling began to grow on what's now our farm. By the close of the Civil War, ignored by the tramping feet and perhaps nurtured by the blood of the soldiers, this seedling would have grown to a modest thirty feet—one of many thousands in a vast troop competing for space in the canopy, biding its time, waiting for the weaknesses of other trees to manifest themselves before taking its rightful space.

At the turn of last century this particular white oak would have approached sixty-five to seventy-five feet, closing in on its mature height of ninety feet. But it would have another full century and more to add to its girth. Nourished by a taproot plunging deep into the earth and undisturbed by the butchery of men in distant lands, the arrival of the car, the plane, and the tractor, this tree methodically put on growth, skinny rings in the lean famine years and fat, upper-class belly rings of indulgence in the feast years.

A survivor of countless storms, the tree stayed put when others failed. Not some flighty understory sprout that rose and then fell back in mere decades, not the grand, fast-growing tulip poplar, this white oak was the mighty burgher of the woodland village. Stolid.

An active participant in staying put, it constantly moved. A casual glance down the driveway found our gauge of the weather. With each breath of wind, the twitching and bending of its smaller branches in dance informed us of the tempo of the music.

When on that day an average thunderstorm rolled across the opposite ridge, when out of the thousands of lightning strikes one sought out this tree, our tree, was there any conscious awareness of death, self, family, loss, and the endurance of nearly two centuries? Was there a sense of submission to a greater power or hubris that this couldn't happen to such a mighty oak?

In the end it was an honorable death, a long life that fell to a greater axe than mine, that random but predictable shaft of wild energy—an act foredestined nearly two centuries ago, that all the mighty and the low will eventually fall.

It was late afternoon when I stopped at a friend's farm. An invitation to sample three new homebrews and some freshly sliced prosciutto from a two-year-old ham had been issued. The short drive found me passing dozens of small homes and farms. None of them could be called going concerns. Most had vegetable gardens and chickens, some had fighting cocks staked to huts, many had a steer in a small pasture and a pigsty near the barn, and one had a gutted buck draped from a pickup truck. These are the features of this landscape. It's a traditional one of people eking by, doing for themselves, not quite the self-sufficing farms of old, but closer than most in this modern world.

In the 1930 census one-third of subsistence farms were in Appalachia, accounting for most farms in the region. Those farms generated less than $100 a year, produced more than 50 percent of their needs on the land, and bartered and traded for the rest in an essentially cashless network. In a system hallowed by custom, kinship, shared work, and shared deprivation, the Appalachian hill people still led a life rich in music, folkways, food, and craft.

Cashless networks create challenges within a capitalist economy. That is, communities operating outside the prevailing system are viewed as a challenge and need to be brought within the sheltering embrace of improvement, progress, and markets. A people not in search of the civilizing influence of a cash economy will be given it anyway. And once it's presented, they'll often surrender to it, for after all the allure of cheaper, plentiful goods is hard to ignore when there is money to spend.

The thirties were really the midpoint in a long and complicated pursuit of bringing progress and wages to the mountain people. That pursuit ultimately resulted in the destruction of those self-sufficing farms and their cashless society and culture. What remains today is a shell, a dependent people, and only the faintest ghostly echo of that former world.

Perhaps it is my romantic streak, but I see ghosts, ghosts of what we have lost in our drive for progress and shiny baubles. One North Carolina woman, at the brink of the Civil War, anticipated the loss to come in that conflict: "How quietly we drift out into such an awful night, into the darkness, the lowering clouds, the howling winds, and the ghostly light of our former glory going with us to make the gloom visible with its pale glare."

How quickly a rural traditional society unravels, one outside paycheck or charity at a time, leaving a pale glare to light the path behind.

We find it hard to step outside our immediate desires and see the long-term consequences. We bemoan the loss of kith and kin, praise the handmade, the local, yet undermine all by our gluttonous drive for new markets and consumption. Left behind is the debris of formerly stable societies, slathered now with the cheap sugary pink frosting of hope and mountains of discarded plastic toys.

On our farm we don't lead a self-sufficing life. We try. But even with our table loaded each night with food sourced from just outside the door, with a pantry full of jars of preserves and pickles and other produce from the garden and orchards, with bacon, jowls, and hams under the stairs, we conjure only a pale outline of what was or could be. We try to barter and repair the literal and figurative fences in our community. But we fail. Those links to a self-sufficing life are now severed. We are too plugged into this economy, too enamored and too reliant to envision a way out.

The problem is not just the fossil-fueled lifestyle, the globally connected train of goods and services, or the commodification of all physical aspects of our modern existence. It is our mindset. We discard the old with ignorance and shortsightedness and embrace the new without question.

Perhaps we mistake the lowering clouds as security and the howling winds as the sound of contented voices. Yet . . . if the pale light guiding my path leads me to three homebrewed beers and some home-cured prosciutto, then I'll gladly trudge on.

It always seemed cold on the Louisiana marsh when I was a boy. On Thanksgiving eve my father and I would drive out to the hunting camp, a ramshackle building under centuries-old live oaks. At dinner we'd sit down at a long communal table and enjoy hearty bowls of duck gumbo. The dozen or more men gathered there would talk, and we the sons would keep quiet, seen but not heard. The morning smell of bacon and eggs served as an early alarm. And by 4:30 a.m. we were climbing into motor-driven mud boats and heading off across the marsh. At regular intervals a father and son would disembark into a smaller wooden pirogue and push off into the darkness, usually arriving at a duck blind an hour before sunrise. Our hunt would begin with my father calling the ducks, enticing them to circle and land.

Come late morning the hunt would end and we'd return home, pulling into the driveway around noon. Thanksgiving preparations inside were already well underway. Pies lined the counter, and I'd cast an anxious gaze to determine that a favored sweet potato pie was among them and then head off to shower and change into clean clothes. The table set and bellies growling, we'd sit down to eat dinner mid-afternoon. Afterward the calls would begin from distant relatives.

As a grown man I have changed my rituals. I'm now the relative calling across the distance of a time zone and 700 miles. Instead of a duck hunt early Thanksgiving, my morning is filled with chores—feeding pigs, sheep, cattle, and chickens, stacking wood for the woodstove. Busy, but still time will be made later for a woodland walk on the farm. We eat late, so no need to rush dinner preparations. Some years we are graced by the company of friends, and other years just the two of us dine.

I'll prepare a roast duck or goose in memory of those boyhood hunts with my father. And I'll regret the absence from the table of a sweet potato pie. But since it is Thanksgiving, I'll be grateful for reasonable health, a loving partner, a satisfying life, a full library, the memories of my father, and a large abundance of siblings and other kin. I'll also be thankful for what is absent in my life, namely, the darkness of war and the dislocation from hearth and home of the refugee.

As I step out onto the porch before sunrise Thanksgiving morning, the air will smell of smoke from a dozen farmhouses in our valley. It will be cold on our farm here in the hills of East Tennessee. The cattle will begin to bawl. But over their din, if I listen well, I will hear the sound of my father calling the wild ducks out on the marsh.

Hearing: When the fog comes into the valley, the cattle bellow an alarm at the loss of a horizon. It's a sound that raises an atavistic fear of the husbandman worried for his stock. You cock your head, desperate to locate the sound. Is this the sound of your own cattle, now escaped and on the highway? An experience lived once stays forever.

Smell: Walking at midnight among the cattle on a sweltering summer's night, you take in the sweet rich aroma of sweat and grass dung rising from the earth—not unlike the smell of yeast and dough working together in a bowl under a heavy cloth. Both are a promise in the dark, a womb-like gift of fertility for those capable of interpreting and understanding their uses.

Touch: While the ewe is still expelling the afterbirth, you cradle her newborn lamb. That small heart beating, that softness, delivers in an instant the totality of life, what the world offers: this mere moment between birth and death and the joy in its living.

Sight: The blood comes quickly, more than you expect. A merciful cut drawn across his jugular, the yearling ram lamb bleeds bright on the winter grass. You carry his dead weight across the barnyard and hoist him up by the gambrel tendons to a singletree dangling from the tractor's front end loader. You pull the hide off and execute the evisceration quickly, then place the carcass in the cooler.

Taste: You place a sliver of smoked pork in your mouth. The fruit of your land, it is simply seasoned with salt and pepper and stuffed with garlic from the garden. The fat is rendered during a long summer day spent in the smoker, then the meat is pulled, chopped, and doused with a vinegar sauce. You serve it on a plate alongside crowder pea salad. You wash it down with homemade mead and wine, sitting around the long table with friends as the day becomes evening. This is farming.

It's time for a confession. Do not trust me with your pocketknife, for I have lost another one. It was a handy little French grafting knife from Opinel. It is easily and inexpensively replaced, but it replaced a more expensive Le Theirs pocketknife, which replaced a German pocketknife, which replaced another in a long line of perfectly good (or even great) knives.

Try an exciting thought experiment. Put yourself in the shoes of this farmer. Or make that a pair of rubber Wellingtons, because it is raining or snowing or icing. You are driving the tractor. It is sliding this way and then that as you make your way up the hill pasture. Ahead the cattle are once again bawling, waiting for fresh hay.

In preparation for dropping off the hay you first must remove the baling string surrounding the round bale. You climb off the tractor, in the rain or whatever, and pull your pocketknife from where it has been nestled securely in an overall pocket under a barn jacket or a raincoat. Reaching up to the bale that dangles from the hay spear, you cut the strings. And here is where it happens.

In the rain or whatever, as the cattle gather 'round impatiently, you do the following: Once you've pulled the various cut strings off the bale, you place the knife on the fender well of the tractor and you get back on the tractor and drive off. You will find this an extraordinarily effective means of losing a knife.

Then there's a second option (my personal favorite). In this scenario, you fold up your knife and slide it into the raincoat pocket. And your knife vanishes immediately and forever, because every farm raincoat has two fake pockets. These are the slits that allow you to reach inside your raincoat and under your barn jacket to access your pants pocket and remove the knife in the first place. By returning the knife to the raincoat pocket slit, you have conveniently deposited it directly into the muck, rain, or whatever for eternal safekeeping.

You never notice its absence immediately. You assume it is in another coat, in a different pair of jeans, on the kitchen counter. But as days turn into weeks the reality becomes clear. You've done it again. So, does anyone care to lend me his pocketknife?

The wind is out of the northwest, the temperature hovering in the low forties, as I hoe the potato beds for a spring planting. A weak March sun breaks through often enough to bring out the ruddy freckles of my hands, hands that are the mirror image of my father's.

At the end of the row I stop and put the hoe away and go inside. It's time to begin packing for a trip home to Louisiana to visit my dad in the hospital. My father is just shy of his eighty-ninth birthday and has always enjoyed good health, but he has had a stroke and is now recovering in a rehabilitation unit. With good care and the attention of my sisters he is in good spirits and improving ahead of expectations.

A couple of days later I am at the hospital, helping him tear open a packet of crackers as we catch up on his progress. Earlier this morning, while he was busy with rehab, I went to the parish documents office to get a copy of my birth certificate. Staring down at the record before me, I was struck by the inheritance that comes with being the son of William H. Miller of Lake Charles, Louisiana. Fifty-three years earlier I was born in the same hospital where my father now recovers. It is the same hospital where all eight of his children were born, the same hospital where my mother and older sister died and where a younger brother passed away a few days after his birth. It is the same hospital where my dad recalled carrying me as he walked up and down the hallway when I was sick as a child.

My cousin from Texas shows up for a visit just as my dad is eating lunch, part of a steady stream of well-wishers who stop by throughout the noon hour and into the early afternoon—an appropriate testament to a man who for most of his life has been an active part of a community, a man who over the years has lent his hands, as it were, to whatever has been needed.

That involvement in the community was a lifelong occupation of my father's generation. Countless hours each week, often on the heels of working all day, were spent in service. Years ago, as a child, I found a handwritten list from my father's boyhood, a list of items he deemed essential to a good life. Top of the list was to do a good deed each day without the person on the receiving end being aware of it. No chest thumping, no look-at-me, just a hidden hand helping others up.

As I prepare to say goodbye and return to Tennessee, I recall an evening when my older brother and I sat around the kitchen table with other family members. We both had our hands resting on the table's surface in front of us. My niece, my brother's daughter, looked across the table and said in surprise, "You both have the same hands!" I laughed and pointed at our father, who was sitting in a similar pose: "Well, there is the template for those hands."

It is those hands I shake as I say goodbye, cognizant that my inheritance is both a privilege and a responsibility.

Oh, how I yearn for the return of the meat-and-three and the simple joy of knowing that with a quick turn off the highway to any small town in the South you could find a diner that served up the sacred trifecta. That assurance brought comfort to restless dark nights.

The daily break for lunch and the communion with one's people have given way to the blight of Hardee's and its ilk, the undiscriminating herd inching forward at the drive-through, devouring at the wheel, afterward pitching leftover hamburger wrappers out the windows. Our collective soul has been starved, even as our collective waistline has expanded.

We were a people of the garden once, the content of our favorite diner's lunch fare reflecting the abundance of the seasons. Served in modest portions that allowed us to eat healthy, but not to excess or somnolence, the choices were varied and yet consistent: two or three meats, perhaps six or more vegetables. The daily decision was made while waiting for the iced tea to arrive.

The chicken was a smaller bird, the cuts done to maximize the number of servings. Each breast was cut in half, and when it was served on the smaller plate of its time it did not dwarf the other choices. The meatloaf was divvied into modest squares, the country ham shaved in thin slices, the vegetables simply prepared with minimal seasoning.

"Yes, ma'am, we are ready to order. Hmm, I will get the chicken today, dark meat, please. And let me have the okra and stewed tomatoes"—which still counted as one side—"turnip greens, and the crowder peas."

"Roll or cornbread?"

"Cornbread, of course."

And when the plate was clean: "Can I get you anything else?"

"No, ma'am, that is all today, no dessert for me."

"No peanut butter pie?"

"Oh, that's tempting, but no, thank you."

"Y'all have a good day then. We'll see you tomorrow."

It is still a couple of hours before sunrise; the birds are chattering in the crape myrtle as the sky begins to lighten over the eastern ridge. Our rooster has been offering up his dawn greeting for at least two hours. And our stockdog Becky just killed a large raccoon at the garbage can.

We have a full couple of days before us planting grapevines and a new nut orchard, adding to the pawpaw grove, finishing the new raised beds for the strawberries, and stretching a hundred yards of fencing. There will be a hard freeze tonight, and preparations will be needed to protect the figs that are fruiting. And I am smoking a whole lamb today for friends who will dine with us this evening.

The workload on the farm in springtime is never-ending. In addition to all the usual chores and ongoing infrastructure projects, the seasonal tasks of mowing, gardening, mulching, and pasture renovating, and the annual job of barn cleaning keep stacking up. Even the simple prospect of getting off the farm for an hour sends us into a tailspin, leaves us feeling that we just got that much further behind.

But for all that work and the accompanying carping, we love this life. The sheer loveliness of spring in East Tennessee, the excitement of waiting for Petunia to farrow, and the pleasure of sharing with friends the bounty of the farm are ample compensations.

Time to get back to it.

The tall grass stings my legs like dozens of tiny, angry, invisible bees. I am reclaiming a 200-yard stretch of two-line electric fence that temporarily subdivides our eight-acre bottom field into two-acre parcels. The large transmission lines that cut across our farm overhead release enough electricity to create a mild current between the damp growth and my bare legs.

Each week our sheep graze the new grass of one of the smaller parcels before we rotate them to the next. Each previous parcel lies in distinct states of regrowth, like snapshots between haircuts taken over time. On this hot, humid afternoon the sheep have retired to the barn, while I, their obliging servant, walk the line with a large reel, cranking the handle slowly to rewind the braided wire.

The job is necessary but tedious. I turn the crank and turn the crank and turn the crank and then, stooping, unhook the braided strand of wire from each of the fifty plastic posts aligned across the pasture. The first long strand collected, I turn back and begin reeling in the second, eventually returning to the starting point, where, the task completed, so is my day.

Soaked in sweat, I trudge back up the hill to the barn and put the spool of wire away.

Earlier in the day had found me spending a couple of hours in the hoop-house. Swigging water from a large jug every fifteen minutes (the garden structure's thermometer registered a toasty 105 degrees), I prepared three new beds for the next rotation of vegetables.

We use a micro-irrigation system to water the hoop-house plants. The driplines are connected to a four-cistern setup that harvests rainwater from our hay-barn roof. A one-hour drip into the soil depletes the water in the cisterns by a third. We water every five days, which gives us a fifteen-day supply of water. That gives us decent odds that a good rain will replenish the coffers. But, in the event of a drought, we also have an underground line fed by a deep well from which we can water the livestock and the plants.

Having returned to the house after reeling in the electric fence wire, I settle in on the front porch with a well-deserved end-of-the-day beer to watch the late evening moving in. Out in the bee yard, Cindy has been adding a honey super to one of the hives. As I watch her walk back up the drive, her face red and her bee suit drenched, I imagine that in this heat working in the bee yard is much like working in the hot hoop-house . . . dressed in a suit and tie and hat.

I sit in my Adirondack chair, beer in hand, and I eye her warily as she approaches. She lingers with purpose at the top of the steps, clearly preparing to alter the course of my idyll, because it is a truth universally acknowledged that a man in possession of a cold beer must be in want of a fresh task. Sure enough, on cue, she channels her inner Jane Austen and says, "If you have a minute. . . ."

4

Terce

THE MID-MORNING OFFICE IS *a sun office and the heart of the workday on a small farm. It is the sweat-of-the-brow, hands-in-the-dirt, muscle-to-the-posthole-digger time of day, the time to get it done and not waste time. Putting my hands in the dirt, I plant, weed, and thin. Dirt, the alpha and the omega: it's where we all begin and where we all end.*

I clean out the barn and pile the manure and bedding. By tomorrow the pile will be smoking, a steam of decay already beginning new life. The farm in action is a plumed phoenix, flaming through life and death and life. Risen from the ashes, the bird becomes dinner, becomes compost and manure, becomes vegetables. Becomes a trinity of yesterday, today, and tomorrow. Becomes us.

Yesterday two friends joined me in cutting several logs into lumber. The morning was spent in pleasant labor, strenuous but never exhausting. Labor that if done in solitary might have been a chore was lightened by their company. Sawdust lay thick on the ground when our work was done, already becoming something new and different, yet still the same.

The challenge of today is to decide in the tomorrow how to best use this tree, this kith of the woodland—this matter, present at the beginning, that chanced to become a tree in a fencerow and became stacked lumber in my shed. My responsibility now is to make something if not beautiful then certainly functional. William Morris had it right, though we have drifted far enough into the fog bank that his words are now muted across the water:

TERCE

"Have nothing that you do not know to be useful, or believe to be beautiful."
It's a directive bold enough to color my sins of misuse scarlet.

We are part and will be part of the plumage of the phoenix that fires and dies and is reborn.

Holding that image in the eye, I will follow Morris's instruction with the lumber. But for now, I start with my hoe, making my rows clean and productive, leaving the plants in fertile soil to track the sun across the sky.

The day will come when this matter too becomes compost and begins again in dirt and life, when trees, in feeding, embrace the sun that brought me to their dark feet.

Finished, I hang up my hoe.

There is a moment that comes every year when the heat and humidity kill all ambition on the farm. I stage a coward's retreat inside, where the air conditioning wages war with the mighty forces beyond the walls.

The blasting furnace outside is best experienced with quick raider's forays made in small bursts of committed energy. My own response to the heat is mirrored by that of the pets and livestock. The cattle emerge from the woods just long enough to traverse the pasture for a much-needed drink in the pond. There the catfish have given up emerging from the cool bottom muck until the seasons change.

Upon hearing the door to the house open, Becky, our farm dog, leaves the cool concrete in the workshop to stare out the door and assess. Do they need me? She clearly would rather stay put. But should I be an Englishman who ventures out into the midday sun, she will gladly be my mad dog and join in the folly.

The hogs, even the ones in the woods, spend their days lying on the cooler dirt under trees or in the wallows. Mud-coated, they seldom arise even when I come bearing buckets of feed. A snort of acknowledgment, a shrug of massive shoulders, and they burrow deeper into the muck with a reasonable confidence that the feed will still be there when the sun goes down.

Confined at night, the sheep have little choice but to graze during daylight hours. But gone are their enthusiastic bursts from the barn in the mornings. Instead, they cluster in cliques at the door as I open gates to fresh grass. "After you." "No, after you!" they bleat before grudgingly crossing the corral to the pasture. Once there, they feed in brief gorgings before falling back in a controlled withdrawal to the shaded sanctuary of the barn. Their pantings, like so many muffled drums—humph, humph, humph, humph—are steady and insistent and do not subside until long into the evening.

Heat-sapped hens with parted beaks panting stand in the shade of the maple. They mirror most closely how we feel, their wings held out from their sides much like we would flap a sweaty garment to stay cool. The rooster, his heart not really in his job, makes a few obligatory attempts at coupling. No doubt firing more blanks than bullets in the heat, he finds few partners willing to submit to his brief embrace.

Armed with the instinctual knowledge that all domestic life is locked in a listless stupor, the red fox in the nearby woods has taken the opportunity to pluck an unsuspecting young chicken from the pasture in broad daylight, providing a nice meal for its kits. A minute later my obligatory dash from the house with shotgun in hand ends with a random desultory blast into the undergrowth, the fox no doubt long gone.

Like the catfish retreating to the muck, I return to my cool study, where, with all ambition withered, I check the calendar, willing it to be any month later than July. I close the shades and lay my head on the desk and resolve to hibernate until fall.

My bookishness, my Louisiana childhood, my habit of looking at a rooster at the end of his procreational contributions and seeing a pot of coq au vin—sometimes I feel the odd duck in this East Tennessee valley. But what I and my neighbors do share is a respect for the land, work, community, and the pleasure that comes from doing for yourself.

The homes in this valley are modest, many built piecemeal. Their yards are strewn with the debris of a wasteful industrial world. But one man's trash is indeed another man's treasure. Tell a neighbor that a weld broke on your bushhog, and he immediately rummages around in the weeds before emerging with a stack of metal slats from an old bedframe he salvaged from a scrap heap ten years earlier. "These should do the trick," he says, then helps you weld the bushhog back together.

This is a poor but resilient rural landscape, one inhabited by multigeneration hardscrabblers seeking only privacy and independence. Chickens, a pig, and maybe a cow are common even on an acre or two, and often a well-tended garden of tomatoes, okra, and pole beans sits alongside the house or shed.

In our valley neighbors seldom call a specialist to fix the plumbing or dig out a clogged septic line. They repair tractors, mend fences, wire a barn, butcher chickens, cure hams, make wine, deal with an intruder (when it comes to wandering dogs, one elderly neighbor adheres to the three S's: shoot, shovel, and shut up), or employ any of the thousands of other skills essential to living a rural life. They do it all themselves or shout over the barbed wire fence for help.

A neighbor may help you run the sawmill for an afternoon, accepting payment in a few beers, conversation, and the side rounds from the logs for firewood. When you step into the neighbor's hot summer kitchen, you may find the occupant hovering over the stove canning endless jars of garden produce. Sometimes you'll come home to find homemade loaves of bread, a jar of jam, a bottle of fruit wine, or a basket of vegetables leaning against the front door.

For better or worse, our neighbors have a yeoman's obstinacy to rules and regulations and change. Even after a couple of hundred years (or maybe because of it), they still do not take to outside government intervention with enthusiasm. They prefer to be left alone to live in a manner that has been repeated through the generations.

This valley is certainly not unique. Across the continent rural values of community, cooperation, and resilience, while battered, still have life. Perhaps we are fortunate that while the urban centers still glow pink-cheeked with wealth, the rustics have more or less been abandoned to muddle along and do for themselves. It's that abandonment that has preserved and nurtured self-reliance and partnership.

Definitely not painted-picture idyllic, their way of living is that of resourcefulness often born of imposed frugality. But it is one model, of sorts, that offers an emergency plan for the rest of us to follow in the hard times to come. Further, a modest people without the capital resources necessary to strip mine the future for their benefit is a gift that this planet might appreciate at this juncture in its 4.5 billion years.

Perhaps it is barn envy. This farm has never had enough structures for the equipment, animals, forage, and tools to meet our needs, despite our ongoing efforts. Years of building hay sheds, equipment sheds, chicken coops, and well houses have provided me with a fair sense of the work, skill, material resources, and neighborly assistance needed to construct those larger hay barns that dot our landscape. So I feel a particular sadness watching old barns falling into disuse or being torn down before their time, the wood destined to deck a second home on the lake or, more often, simply be bulldozed and burned.

Often this tear-down is done by new owners seeking the "country life." The country life is a consumer choice, bought and sold. It's quite distinct from the agrarian life, which is a life of work and provision. In the past five years I have watched two different neighbors tear down perfectly good barns and burn the lumber. One neighbor bulldozed a two-story hay and tobacco barn and replaced it with a poorly constructed lean-to for lawn-mowers and weedeaters and leaf blowers. The other leveled a barn built of American chestnut so his family could create an Olympic-size volleyball court.

A recent conversation with an extension agent about fencing revealed a similar pattern. According to his statistics, more than 50 percent of fencing in our county has been torn out in the past twenty years.

The destruction of an infrastructure that is still perfectly suited to the continued productive use of these East Tennessee valley farms is concrete evidence of the demise of a formerly vibrant community of neighbors and families. The tobacco barn and smokehouse, the chicken coop and milking parlor, all helped to explain who went before and what worked on this land.

Although not necessarily wed to our predecessors' choices, we'd be wise not to wholly ignore them either by tearing down the evidence of their accomplishments. That evidence is a blueprint linking the past to a possible future. Because far deeper than the grain in the wood is the pattern that sustains life and community.

Cresting the hill on my tractor on a summer's evening of bushhogging, I am followed by a long, dry cloud of chaff and dust. Ahead of me lie a few hundred yards of brown fields that extend to the woods. It has been a dry year (technically a moderate drought) that has gripped our valley. It is a claim that in this year of extraordinarily heavy rains or continual rains in many areas of the country seems oddly boastful.

Making the final turn at the bottom of the hill, the south end of the field, in the shelter of the oaks, I find my green pasture. Like the last of the snow left in the shade of a tree, here lies a swath of grass, no more than five yards across, still exhibiting the trademark signs of life.

As a boy in Louisiana I saw my first snow at the age of four—a remarkable day in which the white stuff melted almost as fast as it fell. I ran around our yard, gathering snow from underneath the trees, trying to collect enough to make a snowball. Eventually I brought a golf ball-size ice ball inside to proudly show off. That is what I feel like doing upon spying the patch of green. "Look, Cindy," I say, "green grass. Quick, get a vase before it loses its color."

Tonight finds us driving to another farm the next valley over. Turning onto a small county road, we pass the spot where one enterprising local farmer raises fighting cocks for that lucrative blood sport. Hundreds of wooden huts, each housing a single tethered rooster, are positioned in neat grids up and down the well-manicured hill.

A bit farther and we arrive, across a small bridge over a diminished stream, at the farm of our friends, two brothers, where the next several hours are spent deconstructing four sides of hogs into usable cuts of meat to stock the farm's freezer. In a slightly chaotic assembly line, I focus on separating out the ribs and sides (bacon) and deboning the hams. One of the brothers removes the loins and cuts the Boston butt from the picnic shoulder roasts. Cindy and the other brother take on the job of vacuum packing the massive piles of meat. Meanwhile, our hosts' mother keeps busy presenting trays of snacks and penning content descriptions on the sealed bags of cuts. We eventually head home after capping off the butchering session with a late-night dinner and glass of wine.

The following afternoon we drive back up our dry valley to another farm, where we join a hundred or so guests for a pig-pickin' party. The 200-pound pig is from our farm, bought by a neighbor just this week, then killed, scalded, and slow roasted for thirteen hours. The resulting meat is something any Southern boy would be proud of producing. That it is prepared by a native New Yorker shows that the art of the slow-roast pork is not defined by the geography of one's birth.

After a few hours of conversation and food and accolades for raising such a fine pig, we return home up the long dusty drive, past the dying fields and drying ponds, where the cattle and their newborn calves kick up their heels over some pleasure unseen by us.

It is a cool forty-eight degrees as I step off the back porch. The sun is below the eastern ridge, a heavy dew hangs on the grass, and a light mist floats in the orchard. The crabapple, looking with all its bright red balls like a carefully decorated Christmas tree, is heavy with fruit. There are still figs ripening on the fig trees, and as I bring feed to Peggy I part the curtain of leaves and look for fruit, flicking softly each ripened fig to dislodge other guests. I pop a soft, plum-colored fig into my mouth, then open the gate to feed the sow.

Peggy is up quickly, a sure sign that after a difficult week her appetite has returned. She follows me to the feeding trough, submitting to a quick back scratch as I present her grain-and-slop breakfast. Her piglets burrow down in the hay awaiting her return.

The farrowing began a few evenings back with one piglet and then a long, anxious hour of nothing. Come five o'clock Cindy and I soaped up, and each took a turn at inserting an arm into the birth canal in an attempt to feel for stuck piglets. At 5:30, our efforts having failed, we hit the panic button and called the vet. Nearly four hours later an exhausted sow and vet had delivered seventeen active piglets. In the ensuing days three were lost when Peggy laid on them. Typically a very careful mother, she was undoubtedly much less attentive than usual because of the pain, swelling, and fatigue of the prolonged assisted delivery.

I exit the side gate of the farrowing pen next to the newly erected hoop-house. It is only 7:30 a.m., and the winds are still quiet. In just a few hours a group of friends will arrive to help stretch the plastic over the metal-and-wood skeleton. The completed 24-by-50-foot structure is earmarked to grow our winter crops, and soon I'll be hustling to get the ground prepared and greens planted for fall.

Entering the inner corral I open another gate. It squeaks too loudly and alerts the inhabitants of the barn of my arrival. Out pours our flock of sheep, all eighteen ewes, thirty-six offspring, and one very jealous ram. The ram's recent arrival has made what was formerly a peaceful walk among the flock an occasion for high drama. He emerges from the barn like a gun-slinger to face me down in the dusty barnyard. His head shakes, he grunts, and he takes a few quick steps in my direction. Sidestepping, I slip past him and hurriedly fling open the gate to the pasture.

The cattle catch sight from the lower fields, and their bellows echo off the surrounding hills. Taking the racket as its cue, the sun emerges over the ridge and illumines all of the valley. I turn and walk back to the barn and fill up a bucket of feed for the cattle. It is not needed, but feeding them every few days keeps them docile and eager to come when called. It's measure of control that will be rewarded should they ever escape onto our highway.

A gesture to Grainger and he jumps in the truck for the ride down the drive. With four muddy feet he plants his mark across the entire span of the truck seat. At the double gates that lead to the lower pasture I climb out, bucket in hand. Opening the gate is always a feat with a mob of 1,500-pound cows crowding 'round in anticipation on the other side. I manage to squeeze through and fill the trough with feed, spending a few minutes watching the calves dart in for milk while their mothers are otherwise engaged.

Back in the truck and up the long drive, I pull up to the barn. Grainger tumbles gracelessly out in all of his late-puppy glory. The chickens, meanwhile, have come off the roosts, so I toss them some scratch and layer pellets. The newly hatched chicks are huddled under the heat lamp and barely acknowledge my presence.

One last chore: I walk out to the woods and fill more buckets of feed for the waiting market hogs. They average 225 pounds, with another six weeks to go before slaughter. But I do not speak of such things as I turn the buckets into the trough, and they seem unconcerned that their desire to eat until stuffed might impact the course of their lives.

I leave them fat and content and go back to the house to join Cindy in a cup of coffee. We discuss the upcoming day, and after feeding myself I head back outside.

Sitting in a large tent at a sustainable agriculture fair, I watch as a butcher demonstrates how to section a lamb into the initial primal cuts. After effectively and efficiently dismembering the freshly killed animal, he asks the crowd if we want him to cleave the skull and remove the brain. A tableful of women up front cheer and chant to proceed with the cleaving. Their response discomfits me, the hooting as if at a sporting event. It is an example of how we have come to deal with death, like in a funhouse mirror, through a distorted lens.

Killing gracefully. How we approach the act, if not with reverence at least with mercy, appears to have gone on an extended vacation. Our species has always butchered. Vegetarians and omnivores, organic farms and CAFOs alike—all are sustained on a pile of corpses.

But while I do accept butchery as the blood price of living on this planet, I do not accept that we should pay with a callous heart. As a farmer I have butchered sheep, pigs, and chickens and ended the life of damaged and dying creatures. As a sometime hunter I have pulled the trigger. But never as a grown man, after kneeling on the ground with a yearling lamb cradled in my left hand and slicing the jugular with the knife in my right, have I jumped to my feet and offered a victorious high-five.

When I was a child the excitement of a good hunting or fishing trip always engendered good-natured bragging and boasting. But never once did my father or anyone else in the party point at a dead deer and say, "Who's laughing now, suckah?" To me such over-the-top gloating is unseemly, unmanly. Yet it's a behavior that seems all too prevalent on today's social media, where a hunting victory results in a jokey, irreverent post before the blood has cooled on the autumn leaves.

Such gratuitous exulting seems an outgrowth of our urbanized world, a place peopled by inhabitants increasingly removed from the costs of their existence, a place where respect and compassion seem to have gone wanting, where too many have wandered too far from the honorable path.

Finding the appropriate note in discussing death, particularly as it relates to farm animals, is difficult. Guests to the farm tend either to focus on the pastoral elements, divorced from the end results, or, like the women pounding the table for a good head-cleaving, engage in coarse talk that cheapens the lives we care for daily ("Ooh, look, bacon!"). Both responses fit nicely into our world of industrialization. It's a world of factory farms and factory-like educational systems, work, and purchases; it's a world in which life is lived on an assembly line of experiences that flicker past for our amusement, detached from the blood and sinew of our animal selves.

Farming has always been an intimate exercise in finding and maintaining a path to where we own the acts that sustain our lives—a path where killing (rather than thrilling) humbles and strengthens a respect for the fragility and value of life.

One of my favorite spots on our farm is not so much a destination as it is a place to pause along the way. Situated between the gates of the upper pasture and the hopper field, it's the highest point on our land, a resting place where I can linger in the shade of a massive white oak and catch a cool breeze. There are many such places here, spots that collect and funnel the elements or provide an island of calm from the same. In this place, on a warm day, as the breeze blows up from the neighbors' field through the hopper field, I'll turn off the tractor, lean back in the seat, and take a rest.

To my south the upper pasture softly rises and falls across ten acres. At its center is a large dew pond that even in severe drought remains deep. At the southern end lie the handsome fields of another neighbor, and far in the distance, on a clear day, the Appalachian mountain chain is visible to the southeast.

Closer to home I can see the massive roofs of a handful of McMansions towering above the old pine plantations that fed the Bowater paper mill forty miles away. When the pine monoculture grounded on the shoals of a beetle infestation in the early days of this millennium, the paper and pulp giant sold off the degraded land to the overextended, mainly couples who engaged in a bit of monoculture of their own and built their dream 6,000-square-foot homes for two. When the bottom fell out in 2007, many of the homes were abandoned unfinished. And today, from the vantage point of my tractor seat, the roofs, like mushrooms after the rain, poke up from the dying pine forest, indicating the presence of a larger organism at work.

This restful spot is not only a collector of cool breezes but also an auditory funnel. Sounds that float to me on a hot day archive the life of our valley: the farmer to the south starts his tractor, the brothers to the east yell back and forth as they repair a long stretch of fence line, the young mother to the north calls out instructions to her daughter in the horse ring—all as roosters crow from every direction, mowers hum in a modern imitation of honey bees, and my dogs yip a sound that tells me a rabbit is giving its mortal best to avoid an untimely end.

When I've taken my rest and am ready to start back to work, it once again occurs to me to erect a bench here, where the fences converge between the fields, my own personal retreat, a place I can visit and while away an hour or two. But I never do, instead opting by inaction to preserve this place as a simple haven for a few stolen moments. Like trying to recreate the magic of a well-remembered conversation, I seem intuitively to know that formalizing this special spot as a designated "peaceful destination" would undo the pleasure I find in a surprise rest from work.

On a Christmas morning it is the tiniest of sounds, yet it stands out from the collection of louder and deeper bleats that surround it. The nervous call of a newborn lamb, wandering, just out of my sight, among the mass of ewes. The flock is huddled out of the rain, inside the barn, but it takes only a shaken feed bucket for the woolen sea to flood out into the corral for the proffered feast.

One indecisive ewe runs halfway out, then is brought up short, as if a cord around her neck has been yanked tight. The lamb bleats again, and another joins in, and the mother is instinctively pulled back to her newborn twins. She still trails afterbirth. The lambs are still wet with blood and mucous, yet they are already standing and look sturdy.

I scoop them up, one in each arm, and flip them over quickly: one boy and one girl. I hold them close to the ground for the mother to see, then, as is my wont, slowly "walk" them to an empty lambing pen. The ewe follows with an attentive eye and motherly bleat. Once inside the pen, she inspects the babies and gives a low chuckle of reassurance. Fresh hay, a little grain, and a bucket of water for Mama, and I leave the babies to nurse.

Other ewes with lambs, in their own pens nearby, begin to vocalize their desire to be fed. I see to their needs and turn my attention to the larger flock, the chickens, pigs, and cattle, finishing my morning chores by turning on the irrigation in the hoop-house.

Chores complete, I pause in the breezeway of the barn. I get down on one knee and place an arm around each dog. We stay like that for some minutes, watching the day arrive, all three of us content for a little peace on this morning. Becky breaks the truce with a growl, and I rise and leave her and Grainger to sort out their own issues. My traditional Christmas plate of blueberry pancakes smothered with Steen's syrup awaits.

The wind is gusting in a low whistle outside my study, blowing snow on the front porch. The mercury reads fifteen degrees, and it's still a couple of hours until sunrise. Today's to-do list has been written: Deliver hay and carry out the usual farm chores. Set up heaters in the livestock watering tanks. Castrate and vaccinate calves, then move cattle to their winter field in the back forty. Dig postholes for the new hog enclosure. And, of course, attend to any newborn lambs that may have been born overnight.

As a boy I loved the idea of winter: the beauty of knee-deep snow, sleigh rides down empty back roads, temperatures so cold that lakes froze, the struggle to build a fire and the penalty of failure, marching along snow-covered trails, trapping rabbits with carefully made snares . . . in short, a complete knowledge of the season gained from reading Jack London and his ilk as a youth who grew up south of Interstate 10 in Louisiana.

So when this Louisiana boy moved to Knoxville, Tennessee, and a few weeks later—January 21, 1985, to be exact—the temperature plunged to minus twenty-four degrees, with twelve inches of snow to add to the joy, I thought I was living my dream. The city seemed liberated from the demands of the day-to-day. Of course there was no real struggle. We could always retreat into our drafty old apartments in Fort Sanders to escape the worst of weather. But there was plenty of room to let the inner kid out to play.

That joy and wonder has been tempered since moving to the farm in 1999. We have had plenty of gorgeous snows and any number of brutal cold snaps. We have had ice storms and been unable to leave the property for a week. But now when I look at the forecast and see that it will not be above freezing for at least four days, that there might be an inch or a dozen of snow, I clap a hand over my inner child's mouth. Because I know what the data mean now. And I know that no boss is going to call me and say "we are closed today." The farm doesn't get a snow day.

Winter on the farm means breaking ice, hauling hay in slick mud and snow, loading hogs in finger-numbing cold, fixing the burst pipe in the workshop because I forgot to turn off the water. It means carrying the rock bar up to the back forty to break the ice on the pond so the cattle can drink. It means that instead of sitting in my chair reading about Shackleton, I have to get out in the damned frigid weather and *be* Shackleton . . . even if only for a few hours.

Yet still, this morning, as I wait for the predawn light, the kid who loved Jack London is awake and waiting to see the beauty of a snow-covered world. Possibly, when the temperature rises above twenty, there will be a walk across the farm. I'll go down a wooded path with the trees frosted in white blankets, listening to the muted sounds of the snowy valley.

But for now I think I'll postpone the walk and the non-essentials of the to-do list and instead sit wrapped in a blanket and read Lansing's account of the trials of the twenty-eight men of the Endurance.

I wipe the afterbirth and muck off my hands onto my coat, then grab the sandwich and take a big bite. After a few bites I put the sandwich on a post and go back to the lambing at hand. Such is the farmer's hygiene, practical and not the least bit fussy.

If we are going out for a social call or dinner, an unthinking assessment takes place in my wardrobe and cleaning rituals. Going to town? I'll have a good shower, put on fresh clothes and clean shoes. Farming friends? I might have a quick wash and stay with what I have been wearing in the barn. Eau de barnyard at a get-together with farmer friends is common and unremarked, indeed, unnoticed.

Sometimes the farm follows me to other venues. On one particular morning, I got up ungodly early, fed the animals, and dashed off to the airport for work travel. I spent most of the day in the close confines of planes before finally touching down. After a long drive to my ultimate destination I arrived at my hotel and dropped on the bed, exhausted.

It was only then that I smelled the distinctive odor of pig manure. My brain was foggy from a full day of travel, but I was nevertheless able to recognize that there were no pigs in my room. Following the odor, I quickly tracked it down to a large clump of Exhibit A on my left boot. I cleaned it off and chuckled, thinking about the poor travelers stuck next to me on a four-hour flight.

A doctor friend of mine says that the farm kids he's had as patients seem to be less susceptible to infections or allergies. Just an observation, not a clinical study, he hastens to point out. His assumption is that daily playing amidst the muck, cleaning out chicken coops and horse stalls, eating fruits and veggies straight from the garden—all serve to build up a healthy immune system.

Compare that to the kid who grows up in the city or suburbs, the kid who uses antimicrobial spray or wipes twenty times a day, never goes outside except to be shuttled from home to car to special event and back, and only snacks on foods that have been properly processed, packaged, and labeled. Is it a surprise that kids today seem to have an epidemic of allergies and immunity-related diseases?

Now I'm not advocating that you adopt the practice of not washing your hands. What I am suggesting is that you consider a little bit of dirt, well, natural. For those of us who live in the country, the smell of the barnyard is simply the smell of life. Nothing to get too fussed about. Just remind me to wipe my boots when I enter your house.

❧

It is 5:30 as I head out to the barn, the light of dawn still a couple of hours away. A few hens, alert to my footstep, jump from their roost in anticipation of an early handful of scratch. Floating above the tree line, in the western sky, the moon is a slender crescent. The sheep are quiet in the barn, the roads empty. Perfect.

Life is at its best when I go to bed on time and wake in the early hours. The world seems both smaller and infinite. Like a fresh-fallen snow, the predawn quiescence holds at bay the bustle of the world of our making. The curtain is pulled back for a while to reveal something less demanding and much more impressive.

As a child in a house full of siblings I'd arise long before the sun to check my trotlines for catfish. That time was mine. Having slipped silently out the door, I'd walk through the dark yard to the dock and climb quietly into the jon boat. A push away with the paddle, no light in hand, and I'd coast into the peaceful winter's morning. I'd hold off using the paddle for long moments, gliding on the smooth surface, to enjoy the solitude. Then, with a few swift strokes I'd aim toward the cypress tree along the edge of the pond.

There was always an excitement in that first moment, when, still not using a light, I would reach into the cold black water for the line and feel it twitch hard in my hands, telegraphing the number of catfish dangling along the hundred yards of its course.

Hand over hand I would tow the boat along the trotline across the pond, a hook hanging every foot. I'd draw in each line until a catfish came boiling to the surface, then continue to pull until the fish hung on the inside of the boat. The smaller ones would be released, and the big fat-bellied ones I'd drop into the bottom of the boat, where they'd thump about, sloshing at my feet.

It usually took an hour to run the lines and rebait each hook. A quiet paddle back across the pond, and I'd take the haul of catfish back to the house and clean them in the light of the kitchen window. My father would usually be sitting with a cup of coffee and the paper when I came inside. I'd put the catfish, two each, in clean empty Guth milk cartons. They'd then be filled with water, labeled, and put in the freezer. There, like ice bricks stacked igloo style, they awaited a spring thaw and fish fry.

These many years later a good predawn ramble or spot of work done in quiet reflection still sets me on the right side when the sun comes up. The workload later in the day always seems lessened if I'm outside in the dark just before dawn—my time when the curtain is pulled back a little, letting in the soft glow of possibilities.

I look on as the last of our Red Poll herd clambers aboard the trailer, bound for a farm in Southern Illinois. One lone steer remains behind, with nothing but ewes and lambs for company. Around the corner the Barred Rocks and Brown Leghorns scratch for bugs, totally indifferent to the leaving. The pigs in their paddocks, still sleeping off their dinner repast, are oblivious to all but dreams of breakfast.

To run a small, diversified farm is to live within the wheel. It turns for the seasons, for the markets, for the climate. We have spent many years planning, building, and repairing the infrastructure to support multiple endeavors, to make the farm resilient, to create and sustain a place where the absence of one species simply indicates another cycle, unremarked in the larger scheme.

Livestock live out their lives here, with their offspring, born, raised, fattened, and slaughtered. Crops are planted, watered, and harvested. Dinners are planned, cooked, and enjoyed. The refuse is gathered, emptied, and composted. Wheels within wheels, seasons within seasons, years within years. Everything is done within a scale that is appropriate to our abilities, our infrastructure, our needs.

Some wondered with the sale of the cattle if we were scaling back, down, in retreat. They deconstructed the act, examined the entrails, to discover more than was presented. But if they had taken a closer look and a broader view, they would have seen a panorama painted over the years, one that continues to transform with each brush stroke.

In that big picture the beautiful snow of winter becomes a distant dream come the dry, hot summer. Chicks in the spring lead to a convivial table in the fall. A herd of cattle is followed by a flock of sheep; a harvest of potatoes is replaced by manure and then a crop of beans. The one true constant in all is the turning wheel that brings the careful observer into active participation.

The small farm is itself a participant workshop of opportunities and dreams. It's a place that, if we will read the cycles, does not scale up or down but continues on in a circle, a place where the new becomes the old becomes the new again, all within a framework of what is reusable, possible, and desirable.

As we live within the wheel we are but fleeting stewards. The farm belongs not to us but to a much more demanding landlady, one who insists on her share of the successes and who is unforgiving of our failures. The panorama she paints is of billions of years rather than a handful of decades. And while capricious in her communications—railing one minute and calm the next—she is nonetheless predictable to a degree. Our challenge is to watch for her moods and take only what she will allow, knowing that when we are done the tenancy of this land reverts back to her.

Perhaps, when compared to all the dancers on the world's stage on that particular day, it was of little import. But, on our farm, last week's mini-blast nonetheless cut a deadly rug through the woods.

This has been the spring of many odd and intense storms: The recent eruption that dropped an inch of rain here and seven inches less than a dozen miles away. The storm whose gusts knocked out power in 800 residences in nearby Kingston, yet hardly sent a breeze down Paint Rock way.

The storm last week was a whirling dervish that came through with such force that the windows and walls shuddered, the trees swayed, and at least one neighbor was left looking for the roof of his barn. It arrived as an unexpected guest late last Saturday night. Rain blowing at the horizontal wetted the front porch wall to the five-foot mark. Our lights flickered and went out for a few hours.

The tempest spent its energy in a fury. It moved through the valley in less than an hour and then petered out over the eastern ridge. The following morning's blue skies revealed no damage but a few small branches down around the house and a porch swept clean of chairs and rug. Only did my walk through the back forty to forage for mushrooms later that day tell the true tale.

Up the lane, in the heart of the wood, four modest oaks, each approaching their century celebration, lay in a tangle across the roadbed—two reds and two whites, branches intertwined as if clutching at each other for support in their last moments.

Farther into the wood, on a west-sloping ridge, lay a giant white oak. Assessing age by diameter is difficult, since trees can stay small for many decades before exploding in growth when the opportunity arises, often at the death of a parent weakened by age or illness. But this oak was twice the diameter of the other trees, fully mature, now laid low by this localized event, this small storm of no consequence.

Across a fence into the upper pasture, on opposite sides of a field, two of the most ancient oaks on the farm lay toppled, majestic sentinels of the forest now sprawled like drunks on a barroom floor. One red and one white, both most likely already anchoring their communities at the nation's founding, they somehow looked out of place, prone instead of upright, in their slow death.

These old ones now await, in a condition of helpless indignity, men who will scramble up their sides, hack off limbs, and saw up their trunks before carting the bits off for the beneficiaries' own purposes—the oaks' final will and testament ignored, that they may lie in the ground they lived on and with for so long, their utility reduced into so many cords of fire-wood and sawlogs and days of labor.

No one will miss them but I and the other residents of the backwoods: I for their solid, reassuring presence as I pull my tractor into their shade for a midday lunch, the squirrels for the massive harvest of mast accumulated on the forest floor, a feast epic in tales to be told through the generations. . . .

They were only seven oaks of varied age on a small farm in a small valley, located in the lower end of one of the ninety-five counties of one of the fifty states of one country on this planet during the Anthropocene. And now they are gone.

We had finished hauling a half-dozen pine logs to the lumberyard. Yet there were still a lot of small branches to pick up. So I told the Kid to pick them up and pile them in a ravine and reminded, "Don't make a meal of it. Come find me when you are done." He nodded in acknowledgment and got to work.

Being told since we were kids that a job is not worth doing unless it is done right has misled countless generations, left them dithering at the crossroads of inaction. A dear friend of mine often chastised her husband for cleaning the house less than perfectly. Perfectionist that she was, she never cleaned . . . knowing in her heart of hearts that it would never measure up.

Now sometimes doing the job thoroughly is important, such as with heart surgery. But (and perhaps this is my Southern sensibility) I'm a 90 percent guy: Take care of 90 percent, and the other 10 typically doesn't matter, even more so considering that the last 10 percent can often take 90 percent of your time.

Learning the balance in completing work or spiraling down an anal-retentive vortex of making nail cozies can be a fine line. It is a process we actively engage in each day on the farm, where the list of items increases minute by minute, windstorm by windstorm. Sometimes even a perfunctory completion is the spot-on amount needed to accomplish the task. The skill and the talent of a good worker is determining when good enough is good.

Yesterday I pruned the new wine grapevines to a central leader, put up the trellis wire, and tied the vines off. I left undone the thorough weeding that was needed and an application of manure and mulch. It was time to move on and rake the hay in preparation for baling today. Sometimes (actually, pretty darned often) not making a meal of it instead of spending too much time on a minor project is the appropriate amount to get done.

It's only ten in the morning, and it must be close to a hundred degrees in the hoop-house. After weeding down one row of tomatoes, cucumbers, squash, and melons, I pause to put my glasses, made useless by the sweat streaming down my face, in my overalls pocket before continuing.

The next row, a first planting back in April, is now laden with tomatoes of all stripes and types. I snack on the ripe cherry tomatoes as I prune and tie up the heavy branches.

Finishing the last row, I harvest a handful of bell and jalapeño peppers before going to the house. In the breezeway of the barn substantial piles of red onions and garlic lie curing. Security against winter want, they provide visions of future stews and gumbos. After a quick stop in the herb garden for a fistful of cilantro, I drop off the produce with Cindy, who is busy making salsa, and return to my next morning task.

I am an avid procrastinator when it comes to weeding and mulching perennials. There always seems to be something more important to do, whether it's trimming sheep's hooves or sitting on the deck with a cup of coffee. But today the looming chore has risen to the top of the list. I finish out the morning by weeding and mulching the grapes, blackberries, pawpaws, and blueberry bushes. As I work I snack, first on the blueberries and then on the blackberries, in a comfortable rhythm. Eat berries. Pull grass. Repeat.

There is a satisfaction in being able to walk the farm and snack or harvest in any season. Whether it is greens in deep January or wild chanterelles in late July, the real "movable feast" is there for the taking (with a little bit of sweat and labor). Even the sassafras trees contribute; I gather and grind their leaves to a fine powder in my annual production of gumbo filé.

Today's munching is just an appetizer for the summer months to come. Soon there will be ripe beefsteak tomatoes, juicy sweet Charentais melons, platters of figs, and salads of peppers, cucumbers, homemade yogurt, and dill—each month's cooking informed by the season, each month with its own theme. Next month is July, and it already has me salivating in anticipation. I'm thinking grilled ribeye with a little salt and pepper, garlicky mashed potatoes, sliced tomatoes topped with fresh basil, homemade bread, and a few glasses of wine for a theme.

This work of farming sure goes down easier if you enjoy the pleasures and conviviality of the table, or just the taste of a warm, fat blackberry on a humid afternoon, plucked from the vine a moment before you pop it in your mouth.

5

Sext

IT'S THE MIDDAY OFFICE and I've brought my chair to the bottom of the two-acre grass-covered bowl, my own private Greek amphitheater on the south end of the upper pasture. The greening spring grass grows thick where the playgoers sit; the stage for the actors and chorus is set hard against a fence, its backstage leading out to a former wood.

Here our play opens and the oracle enters. She sees the fence line we have erected, its feeble suture stitched on the land, and recognizes in it our hubristic claim to own what can't be owned. She sees the future, and the future already knows what we have forgotten.

The backdrop to the play is the clear-cut forest where I used to harvest ramps each spring and chanterelles late summer, deep in its quiet center. Now it lies as an exposed wound of splintered trees and muddy roads, marking a deafness of the present custodians and neighbors to the past and the future.

Stage left is land that until recently belonged to an aging farmer who is in the long process of retiring, step by slow-moving step. He stopped by to deliver some much-needed hay the other day, and I had a chance to chat with him about his life. Had he ever worked with horses? Yes, he said, he used to love to drive a team out into the field to pick up shocks of corn, the rhythmic stooping and bending work he liked as a youth. How old, I asked, when you were allowed to drive that team by yourself? Oh, very young, he responded. Eight years old.

Can I name a child of acquaintance who has the intelligence and maturity to handle a team of horses, the stamina to spend the afternoon doing *physical labor? How sad and absurd that we should think we have improved on the past by infantilizing our children, swaddled even into youth and young adulthood, their girth and limbs malformed, their intelligence maladapted to the work of being men and women.*

On these unsettled thoughts the midday hour closes, and I pick up my chair and walk back down the lane to the heart of the farm. The sounds of the chorus fade. Rounding the last bend, I ignore the muttering of the audience and pretend the oracle's prophecy was wrong. Blinded, I reenter this modern life.

The mercury is already pushing the mid-eighties by afternoon, and clouds are beginning to build in the west. I sit in my car in a Pennsylvania parking lot next to a mattress store, watching. Across a field a boy is perched on the bench seat of a hay wagon, holding the reins to a team of Belgians. Farther back stands an older boy. He is reaching down and catching square bales as they are tossed up to him from other boys on the ground. He already has stacked a layer three high on the sixteen-foot wagon. The driver, maybe eight to ten years old, twitches the reins and moves the load forward every few minutes before again coming to a stop. Up ahead the father is driving a second team that pulls a gasoline-powered baler. It spits bales onto the ground at regular intervals as it tracks the windrows of hay.

The scene I observe is a Hieronymus Bosch painting with a twist: In the background of the tableau the family of man and boys gathers forage for the winter. At the forefront a stoplight blinks commands on a four-lane highway, the center of a tortured world of strip mall architecture, where the tired and the lost pour onto the roads and the pavement groans under bumper-to-bumper traffic. A boy, the same age as the ones working the field, sits in a car, screen-staring his young years away. A man in the front passenger seat stares to the front, oblivious to any other way of living. A Chick-fil-A and an Olive Garden bookend the paved landscape and the fields of the family at work.

Farther down the road, back in the stream of modernity, I pass three different buggies of Amish women, all driving teams, their children aboard, moving down the highway at five to eight miles an hour. If the journey is indeed more important than the destination, then these women and their children have learned the lesson well. They are chatting and laughing as their fellow travelers, mere feet away, are entombed and unsmiling.

Do they ever glance at the cars and wonder, like May Swenson: *Those soft shapes, shadowy inside the hard bodies—are they their guts or their brains?*

I pull into my hotel parking lot, retrieve my luggage, check in, and go up to my room. I open the curtains to glimpse the last of the day. Across another parking lot, across a road, lies another field. In the dying evening light, another man and a team of black Percherons pull a manure spreader across the pastures back to the barn. On the seat to either side of him are his two sons, sharing an unheard conversation.

Standing at the window of the third floor, in isolation, sadness, and cowardice, I think, *We chase our lives across the decades seeking a sense of purpose, yet our gaze is averted from the possibilities and the wisdom gained from living slowly, at five to eight miles an hour.*

I was sixteen when I put brand new brakes on my car. It took most of an afternoon, and it was a task that when finally completed gave me a real sense of accomplishment. True, I had a couple of small parts left over. But I was young and operated under the assumption that the auto parts store had given me either spares or parts that didn't go with my model.

Once finished I climbed in the driver's seat, turned the ignition, and took off down the road. Wow! It was a smooth ride and I felt great. That is, until I came up fast to my first stop sign and applied the brakes. Odd feeling, pushing down on the brake pedal at fifty miles an hour and encountering no resistance. It's a memory I can still summon readily to this day. Fortunate for me, the auto engineers had built in a backup mechanism called the emergency brake, a handy invention that I deduced might be best to deploy . . . quickly.

I give you this preamble as evidence that even though a person comes from solid civil engineering stock, basic mechanical skill is not an inherited gene. We all have the friend, often on speed dial, who is great at teasing out the workings of most any thingamajig. But my solutions to mechanical problems are victories hard won. The puzzles that five-year-olds routinely solve on Facebook in a cute two minutes elude me—sometimes for hours, and sometimes for many years.

The Neanderthals who lurk in my ancestry were a smartish but conservative group of bipeds. They developed a reliable tool kit over the millennia to make their lives run smoother. But then they apparently had a community meeting and said "enough is enough," and they settled in for the next 100,000 years and made no new improvements. I kind of admire that about them. And perhaps we could learn a thing or two from that approach to technology.

But then there is my H. sapiens DNA. It allows me, eventually, not only to see a solution but also to want to implement it. Yesterday, for instance, we were unloading feed barrels. Cindy backed up the tractor and boom pole to the bed of the truck. Dangling from the boom pole was a nifty contraption called a barrel lifter. This simple invention is the best $40 we ever spent. It has a metal "hand" at each end of a chain that grabs the edge of the barrel and a ring in the center that attaches to the boom pole. Once the boom pole is raised, the barrel, clasped in the barrel lifter's hands, swings up and out of the truck bed. No muscling required.

On this day the first barrel was a breeze to unload. The second barrel presented a slight problem. It didn't completely clear the bed of the truck. Taking on my finest Thinker pose, I struggled for a solution. After some minutes "the little gray cells began to sing." It's the weight, I deduced triumphantly! Each 300-pound barrel of feed removed took more weight off the truck suspension, thereby raising the bed of the truck a couple of inches and causing each subsequent barrel to drag along the tailgate when hoisted. But voilà! A few adjustments to the tractor's three-point hitch, which in turn shortened the top link's angle after each barrel was unloaded, gave the boom pole a higher lift. Problem solved.

This eureka moment may not mean much to the engineering types. But small successes like this one are huge to my sapiens self—victories for H. sapiens yet disappointments to my inner Neanderthal, who wrinkling his jutting brow mutters, "What's next? Will he be wanting to invent block and tackle?" Perhaps. But I must leave that astonishing accomplishment for later. I've just had a brain flash that there might be a better way to knap flint!

Dawn: Sitting on the back deck with a first cup of coffee, I contemplate the rain-soaked windrows of hay on the hill in front of me. I had just finished baling half of what would have been a record harvest the previous evening when the storm broke over the ridge, bringing with it heavy winds, rain, and hail. Heading back to the barn on the tractor, I saw a glass that was half empty. Now, in the early dawn light of a new day, I see my work cut out for me: turning over the sodden windrows to let them dry out before attempting to bale the remainder of the hay. The dogs interrupt my thoughts to announce a coyote halfway up the hill. He stares down at his nemeses, separated by a woven wire fence, and abandons the hayfield. "Comrade," I say into the new morning air.

Mid-morning: I rustle a branch, and a mourning dove explodes out of the crabapple tree. Pausing from plucking the ripe red fruits, I lean in on my orchard ladder and part the curtain of twigs and leaves. There, hidden in the heart of the branches, is a single fledgling within days of its first flight. Fat and unlovely, like the son who won't leave home, it takes up the whole nest. It stares at me with one anticipating eye before, in a "you aren't my mother" moment, turning back to its inner world of waiting. I close the curtain and finish my harvest. I return to the house with two full buckets of fruit.

Noon: I toss down the last of the fresh bedding for the lambs, completing one of my more enjoyable tasks on the farm. I'm tempted to collapse into the soft hay but instead grab a bag of mineral salt to fill up the flock's saltbox. Before filling, I turn over the box to knock out the bits of poop and straw—and in the doing uncover a large nest of mice. Dozens of small rodents swarm over my boots and scurry for the barn exits. The dogs jump into action, fulfilling their designated role just outside the barn gate with loud abandon. Inside the barn, meanwhile, two dozen lambs stampede the empty saltbox, obliviously trampling the remaining mice. I quickly replace the mineral salt and then leave the natural order to sort itself out.

Evening: I'm back on the deck, a pint of beer in hand, the drying windrows in front of me. The dogs assume I need convincing of their utility and pick up their pattern of wild barking toward the hill. I rise from my chair and spot a majestic twelve-point buck. He stands in the evening light, the last rays of the setting sun as his company. Ignoring the peasant dogs, he turns and strolls with a dignified air over the hill and out of sight.

Raising my glass, I toast him and the close of another day on the farm.

Winter: It is twenty-four degrees on the morning No. 28 is born. Sleet pellets bounce off my old Carhartt jacket, and the sky is slate gray when I head out on my early morning rounds. The two cups of hot coffee help little in warding off the chill wind as I rush through my outdoor chores before reaching the relative warmth of the barn.

Entering a barn during lambing season involves careful observation. Who is soon to lamb, and is anyone showing signs of a distressed labor? Who has lambed already, and are all lambs up and nursing? The experienced mother will keep close track of her offspring, protecting them from the scrum of other sheep, but a first-time mother is easily unnerved and will often rush outside without her newborns, trailing the afterbirth, oblivious to what is expected of her in this new role in life.

On this particular morning in early January a handful of fresh faces greet me—the most exciting, twins born to our favorite ewe, No. 1333. No. 1333 is a large, handsome ewe who is uncommonly friendly, always standing still to receive a good scratching. As in the previous lambing season, she has just given birth to a male and a female. Much to our disappointment, she lost the last year's ewe lamb in a freak accident. We are especially anxious that nothing go wrong this time.

Later in the day we eartag No. 28 and her twin, 29. In the end we will have finished the season with 44 lambs, but in this first week of the year lambing is just getting started. Beyond the identifying numbers, the twins are soon indistinguishable from the mass of other lambs, running in and out of the larger flock, occasionally pummeling the udder of their mother.

Spring: Unlike the long and devastating drought of the previous year, this winter and spring's rains have created a lush growth by April. It has become a daily event for us to remark on the change in landscape, as the unnatural browns have given way to the deepest greens. The lambs and ewes are turned out on new grass and thrive. For hours on end we watch the youngsters tumbling about in soft grass at play, interrupted only by a mother's bleat or a long, sun-warmed nap. Throughout the season the inevitable deaths occur: the lamb born at night that managed to roll under the barn wall and succumb to the elements outside, the one I had to dispatch mercifully after it was run over by the flock. We only hope that they are a rare occurrence.

Summer: Mild temperatures and steady rain, a record hay crop, and modest garden success provide the backdrop as our little No. 28 transforms into a hardy, large-framed weanling. In June we separate the ewe lambs from their mothers. For the next few days the moms crowd one gate, the lambs another, fifty yards between them, and bleat. Loudly. Day and night. Another couple of days and the moms turn their attention back to the grass; a couple more and the lambs finally follow suit. Weaning accomplished, quiet is restored.

Fall: It is an October evening during the late Indian summer, as we pull down the gravel drive to enjoy an evening with friends, that we spot a lamb lying in the tall grass of the bottom pasture, noticeable by its isolation from the flock. We stop the car and walk out to the field. There she is, No. 28, head up, alert, but unmoving.

Sheep are prey animals. They don't lie down and stay down unless they are physically unable to go anymore. We grab a wheelbarrow, put her in for the ride, and I push her up the long hill to the barn. We secure her in a stall and go on to dinner.

That night we treat her with the first line of defense, dewormer. For us worming is an infrequent occurrence. All sheep have some internal parasites, but we select and cull based on an individual's ability to carry a small enough "worm load" to thrive without repeated deworming. Two days on the young ewe is still down, so we give her an injection of antibiotic.

Over the next few days No. 28 remains alert, yet she is still unable to stand. Each morning we bring a bucket of warm water and mild soap to the barn and sponge off the accumulated scouring (diarrhea) from her rear legs. At this point we begin to suspect an internal injury.

The day before we found her lying in the lower field, our 200-pound ram had managed to breach a fence and spend the night with her and another ewe lamb. Our new working hypothesis is that in the process of breeding the developing young ewe, the ram has caused nerve damage to her spine.

Having ascertained that her back is not broken, we rig up a makeshift sling of saddle girths in hopes of retraining No. 28 to stand. For the next three days, we place her in the sling three times a day with her feet just touching the ground. We exercise each leg, moving it forward and backward, side to side. Through all of this, the ewe lamb continues to have a healthy appetite. We are committed to nursing her as long as the possibility of recovery still exists. But recovery is not to be.

On the morning of the fourth day when I enter the barn, No. 28 is lying upright, but her head is extended forward and her chin rests on the hay. This is never a good sign, yet Cindy and I are both loathe to give up on her too soon. We are anxious to preserve both her genetics and her life. She remains a calm, affectionate lamb, seemingly glad to have her head stroked even in her distress.

I leave the barn and mount the tractor to finish bushhogging an upper pasture. We have a cold front coming in around midday and are expecting rain. It is a few hours before I make my noonday hospital visit to the patient. This time when I approach, the young ewe's neck is stretched out in the hay, her body limp, like a balloon with a slow leak. Her eyes still follow me, but without the usual spark. This is an act in a play that we have seen too many times. She is going to die—it is now just a matter of when.

I walk slowly back to the house. I pick up my .30–30 and return to the barn. The lamb's labored breathing is audible when I open the stall gate. I raise the rifle and shoot her between and just above both watching eyes. She dies instantly.

Outside, the cold rain begins to fall on the valley. I return to the house, gun in my hand, breathing in the smell of the rain, of this season, aware of this rhythm, this awful beauty in the dying of the year. And I look ahead, on another cold day in early January, to when the next lambing season will begin on the farm, always in hope and sometimes in death.

Somewhere—the gravel road I grew up on, the wharf I fished from, the woods at the end of the road where we roamed, the edge of the bayou where we fought off pirates to keep them from landing—is no longer. It is now an anywhere of pavement, sidewalks, a Walmart, hotels, casinos, and housing developments. Anywhere is nowhere.

Anywhere is a global assault weapon, firing bullets of convenience and terminal extraction. Even without a smarter-than-you phone, you can find, around each corner, the Starbucks, the McDonald's, the everywhere of anywhere. All the signs, hovering over expanses of concrete, flashing the conquest-driven desires of the Empire to colonize the somewhere.

It always begins, thus, with the paving of roads. (For we all secretly know, the road in is a road out.) The new road comes to town, and the longtime general store closes down, its population drawn by the seductive pull of the dollar store that opened in the next small town. Then that up-and-coming town gets a check-cashing store, and a rent-to-own, and a doublewide mobile home dealer. In a few years that small town is compacted and consumed, repackaged, and reissued, newly minted as a bedroom community of the anywhere. And its growing population learns the limited joys of spending its days circling the streets of plenty, like water in a drain.

A genius of the Empire is that it was built in bricks of self-loathing. The new construct is a place where the food of one's people is scorned and a quarter-pounder Thai burger sounds like a possibility, where the inhabitants wander around in such dislocation that their limbs move like invertebrates of the sea, clutching at random unneeded objects in a painful effort to perambulate the Costco shopping aisles.

Ultimately, used up and useless as a boarded-up Kmart that becomes a rock band masquerading as a nondenominational church, the Big Show leaves us, pulls out of town. In its wake is a cratered post-battle landscape, a lonely fortified outpost of colonization on the edge of town that pays low wages and serves up a ghost offering to Anywhere. Pale in its incarnation, the orbiting halogen sun flickers just brightly enough to illuminate our dreams. And inside this opium den of our own making, clutching our pipe, we eagerly inhale the fumes and forget, for a while, that we once lived somewhere. That we *were* Somewhere.

The sun hovers on the western horizon, an hour left on its time clock, as I walk out the back door and up the wooded lane beyond the pasture gates. The walk is quiet, muffled by deep leaves of countless seasons on this land. My destination, as it often is: a pile of boulders at the base of a half-dozen oaks. I climb onto the largest and use a smaller, four-foot stone as a footrest.

A cairn of rocks six feet tall and twenty feet across lies at the edge of the pasture. Another stands illuminated across the field like a treasure hoard in the curious light of a low sun through a leafless deciduous forest in November. The rocky groupings are seated on the sidelines of all our pastures. They are hard evidence of generations of boys who spent their youth in farm chores, among them picking up the relentlessly erupting rocks and stacking them in mounds.

Behind me lie two oaks felled by storms decades past and decades apart, one now nearly buried in leaf litter, its long cycle of decay almost complete. Ten yards away a limb as big around as my waist dangles forty feet up. Broken off from a parent white oak, it hangs like that sword above us mortals who dare imagine the world as our throne.

The sound of Cedar Fork Creek is barely audible as it channels under the bridge at Possum Trot. Another quarter-mile and it will narrow at the decaying Cook's Mill, where elder neighbors recall as children hauling mule-driven wagonloads of corn for milling.

A leaf spirals into view, released from a seasonal contract to land at the foot of a massive shagbark hickory. Nearby a deep-rooted sourwood, contorted in the last ice storm, refuses to submit to gravity. At its base a large stone is covered with the debauched remains of a dinner by the resident squirrels, bits of hickory and acorns piled in the center of the table.

A small flock of wild turkeys, feeling safe a couple of days after Thanksgiving, ambles across a lower pasture and enters my wood. On the far side of the road beyond lies the expanse of pastures that marks our neighbor's cattle farm. From there comes the nervous bawling of dozens of cows as they discover their new home after an auction in a nearby town.

Their disquiet competes with the sound of distant chainsaws, from all points of the compass, chewing on wood. And then, unexpectedly, another intrusion. A neighbor beyond the eastern ridge and half a mile away fires up his ATV to begin what is an early start to his habitual late-night motorized rambles.

Toward the house I can just hear Cindy in the woods as she clangs the lid off a feed barrel. An overeager hog squeals as it hits the single strand of hot wire. I smile. I can check the task of determining if the current is pulsing off my to-do list for the next day.

I rise from my perch and turn toward home—not straight down the lane, but at an angle that leads me into the heart of the woods. I note a likely Charlie Brown Christmas tree along the way. I then pause, as is my wont, at a sentinel white oak. Its circumference is all of fifteen feet, its trunk reaches forty straight feet before the first branches erupt, and the fissures in the bark are two inches deep. I lay hands on it, hoping to receive a blessing of sorts.

Now on the edge of the main woods, I traverse a pig paddock not in use. In the middle is a tall pile of fallen limbs. It provides a sometime shelter for the hogs and, more often, a haven for the red fox that ventures out to make raids on errant hens.

By the time I exit the woods Cindy is trudging up the drive in her beekeeping suit, fresh from checking that her charges are well-fed and secured for the cool night to come.

The sun has set, the light fades, and I enter the house, pleased to call it another good day.

It pains me to speak of parental moral failings. Yet an honest, clear-eyed assessment of the shortcomings of our role models is what makes us men and women, separates us from the mere beasts, even when the lessons on how to live are learned at the clay feet of those nearest and dearest. Indeed, out of rigorous self-examination does greatness rise.

Now in order that others gain from such experience, let us draw back the curtain, stiffen our spines, and take instruction. My stepmother, limited by her birth in North Louisiana, had two principal failings, each of which was encouraged by not being instantly and roundly denounced by my South Louisiana father.

The first is that she put a powdered creamer in her coffee. In those distant days when the northern part of the state was still a foreign country, the natives of that blighted land were wont to use this unholy substance. And they did so without shame. When dining at the Pioneer Club, with all the family as witness, my stepmother would request it with her after-dinner coffee. A quick scurrying by waitstaff, huddled conversations, and eventually a distraught chef would issue from the kitchen with apologies: "We are sorry, ma'am, but we do not have this 'powdered creamer.' Would you like some milk?" My stepmother soon took to carrying a jar of nondairy coffee creamer, a scarlet sin hidden away in her purse, for emergencies, its mere presence an indication of membership in an outlier clan of which such an act would be construed as "normal."

The second failing, and perhaps the more to be pitied, was her preference for Smucker's fruit syrups over our native Steen's cane syrup. No doubt my siblings will be mortified at my airing of such dirty laundry, but there it is. It cannot be unsaid. Sins of such magnitude (to be cataloged alongside the predisposition of norlanders to drown their breakfast with sweet tree sap) cannot be lightly dismissed with a "we must make allowances." Lines must be drawn.

That my brothers and sisters have all managed, even with this egregious moral instruction, to still learn, one foot before the other, that a syrup created from the juices of sugar cane stalks cooked in an open kettle to burnt gold is the only correct choice to pour over pancakes must surely give hope to the citizens of our land. Children learn lessons from both good and bad example. They can and do transcend poor practices through acute observation, ultimately choosing the higher road and shunning the moral transgressions of those of weaker constitutions.

Fear of flavor is not a lost moral crusade; pilgrims still struggle on the rocky road. Although in these waning days of the Republic our options may be limited, the way obstructed, we still stand resolute with a courage that never wavers.

Steen's syrup, now and forever.

In the darkness a couple of hours before sunrise, the wind has come up. I dress quietly and find my way downstairs. After making coffee I take a seat in the old Adirondack chair on the front porch. The warm blast in advance of the cold front, roaring in like heavy surf at night, rolls over the wooded ridge and across the valley in waves. Becky, our aging stockdog, takes up point behind the chair, in easy reach of a comforting hand. Obstreperous bulls and boars are as nothing before her snarl, but a bit of rain, a rifle shot, or a clap of thunder sends her from the field in a cower.

Something has shaken loose out by the hay barn, prompting me to mutter a hope that it isn't anything significant. As Christmas draws near, it is not visions of sugar plums but rather vast sheets of plastic blowing off hoop-houses that dance in my head. Meanwhile, the yearling lambs bleat in protest at being awakened. I should tell them that with a month left on this earth, they'd best be up and enjoying the early morning. The butcher waits for no one.

Perhaps the great thread spinners prompted me to do the same this morning—one never knows when death will arrive. On the eve of the winter solstice this year we hosted the daughter of a best friend of mine from college. Only two years old when her father unexpectedly passed away twenty-two years ago, she was now beginning a quest from the Northeast to visit his friends, to answer the unknowns of self and place.

It had been more than thirty-three years since I shot pool and drank Dixie beer in the Bayou with her father. I could hear him clearly in her voice and laugh, reminding me that we only think we are masters of our individual selves. A step back reveals context, threads connecting us as part of a larger and lovelier tapestry. Like the wind hurtling over the ridge, which began over the flat prairie, which began over the cold oceans, we have origins within origins rolling back, back, to the beginning and the before.

On the morning of the solstice we put my friend's daughter in her car. She headed south to a Louisiana home she had never visited, a motherland that had nurtured generations of her father's family. We wished her well and waved goodbye.

And now, this early morning, my coffee finished, the storm moving closer, I rise and bring Becky into the house. She makes a beeline to her safe place behind the venerable Morris chair. The chair is a relic of a wedding suite belonging to my great-grandparents, bought in Boston on their honeymoon, brought home to Crowley, Louisiana, before journeying north to Tennessee, a century later, to this farm of their great-grandson.

I return to the wind and begin my morning chores, my first stop making sure the hoop-house is indeed intact. The pregnant ewes in the main barn let me know with familiar bleats that they wish to be fed and turned out into the fields. The ewes are only days from the start of lambing season, bellies hanging low, udders engorged, the struggles of birthing and raising last year's offspring forgotten in this year's discomfort of waiting for the new generation, fresh threads on life's ancient tapestry.

There is no pretending that this is anything but a misery, walloping a completely frozen cistern with a rock bar in the vain hope of finding water in the depths. Nothing for it now but to return to the house 300 yards away and start lugging buckets of water, two at a time, filled at the hydrant. Stoop, stand, walk, repeat. Three times a trip and three times a day.

This might be a good time to call upon my reserve of latent Scandinavian DNA, that inner vast, untapped, frozen reservoir of stoic resolve. Or perhaps I could mitigate the effects of the cold by cursing like my great-great-uncle, a merchant marine captain legendary for his facility at swearing in the middle of a word. I try my hand. "Miser-damn-able weather!" I say. It is the best I can muster, and it does nothing to thaw the cistern or warm my toes. It does, however, bring a smile to my frozen cheeks.

It's a smile that quickly fades as I peer into the hoop-house. The collards and mustard greens—at a balmy sixty-nine degrees they benefit from the radiant warmth of Old Sol as all outside struggles to hit eighteen—need water. Stoop, stand, walk, repeat, repeat, repeat. Miser-damn-able weather.

I walk the quarter-mile to the mailbox, in and of itself a feat of Shackleton proportions. It's the wind that does me in. Zero, sunny, and calm I can handle. But any wind at eighteen degrees is "in-damn-sufferable." (Eureka, esteemed mariner! I think I have it!)

What I don't have are the seed catalogs. And what I want more than anything, having now accrued enough chill hours for this gardener to go dormant and prepare to bud, is to while away my evenings dreaming of a better garden, one that this year will be free of flea beetles, squash borers, and potato bugs, one that will sport well- and timely mulched rows and neatly trellised crops, receive just the right amount of rain at just the right moments, with temperatures not too hot, not too cold. Not too much to ask.

Even the inestimable SESE (Southern Exposure Seed Exchange) hippies have let me down. Still lost in 1969, they are late in delivering. I imagine the whole collective hard at work, turning the crank on the old mimeograph and hand-stapling the new seed catalog before they all climb into their beflowered VW bus for the annual trip to the post office and the mailing of their excellent offerings.

Fat lot of good their delay does me right now. I could break dormancy at any moment.

The gray days of February have long since settled in over our valley. A round-the-clock mist, drizzle, and downpour greets my every foray to the barn. High blue winter skies are but a fevered dream seen in quick glimpses before being chased away by the cloud lords of the lower realms.

The drip from the trees, buildings, machinery, and tools is as the sound of the crypt: it brings the promise of eternal dampness into these bones. The animals cry out for relief, a dry patch, a kind word from the grumpy caretaker. Yet their squeals and bleats strike no chord before my sodden heart. I wring it out, reducing its size by three, and feel nothing but an urge to get back inside.

There I hang up my coat. It whispers, "I'll clothe you again in dampness when you are ready." Cup of tea in hand I retreat to my study and listen as the drip outside my window holds a conversation with the power lines a quarter-mile distant. It's an exchange of semaphore sizzles, dashes, and drops spoken in a rural dialect I don't understand . . . except to know by the laughter that either I am the subject of much mockery and mirth or, worse, that they are ignorant of my existence.

Outside these walls the sheep have grown quiet in damp defeat, while the cocks shuffle on their roosts and squabble over sleeping partners. The sun has long since dropped below the western horizon, exhausted from a pointless daylong contest with the clouds.

The hour is late, and I add a splash of Islay to my tea. Picking out a book from the stack, I lean back into my easy chair and resolve to wait out the gray overlords. I offer up a silent toast and then a prayer for their banishment.

❋

The front wheels are angled perfectly for the eight-foot gate opening between the barn and the corral. A round bale of hay dangles from the front spear. In spring, summer, and fall the tractor turns smartly, with clearance on both sides. But this is not spring, summer, or fall. The tractor takes on a mind of its own and begins sliding off to the left, back tires pushing forward, front tires mired lug-nut deep in mud until, rudderless in the late winter slurry, it skids to a halt against the gate post.

In the mud season in East Tennessee the weather is never quite warm enough to dry out the ground, and the green grass is still a month away. Every surface is in a stalled-out state between slop and frozen. Margery Fish, in her book *We Made a Garden*, says, if you want to know what the world looked like after the great deluge, visit a barnyard in winter. We say, if you want to visit our farm, wait until spring. Sad sheep paths and nasty pigsties look to those unlearned in the ways of the farm to be the product of gross inattention. And they look the same to me, even though I know better.

Each slippery step I take leaves a rut in its wake, the dead grass sloughing off like a snakeskin with my passing boot. It's as if the world has taken a giant gulp and held its breath until its skin has become soft and spongy.

The sow peers out of her shelter when I approach, her bulk blocking her piglets from the great outdoors: "Not today, kids. You'll just track it all back inside." The hens scouring the barnyard take great shuddering leaps to clear the mire and get to higher ground and fresh bugs. Eggs collected in this season are all imprinted with muddy, spidery claw prints.

Every year 'tis the same complaint. Then every year the mid-March miracle occurs. All in a matter of a week, two at the most, emerald hairs of grass explode from below. The sponge squeezes and even the ruts from the tractor fill in, seemingly overnight. The trees on the opposite ridge wear their first hint of green, and the rose-purple redbuds begin to work their understory magic in the deep woods. Demeter comes out of her funk as her daughter returns.

But for now early spring growth is just a memory and a promise. The tractor tires still mutiny against my commands. They go left when I order right. The mud offers no purchase to my boots. The sheep reproach me with yellow eyes as they leave the barn single file on a high path out of the mire. I back up and try for the gate again, and the rain begins to fall, merging sky with muck.

❧

With the first of two sixty-foot rows of onions in the ground, I send the Kid, who has just started working on the farm a few weeks ago, into the greenhouse. The instructions: Bring me a bundle of onion sets for the next row. After a couple of minutes, he comes back . . . with a turtle shell in his hand.

"Brian, do you think Cindy wants this?"

"No," I replied, "you can have it."

"Cool."

"By the way, did you get the onions?"

"Oh, good lord," he says.

Sometime later, after running a string to guide our hand, we have the second row planted. Donning my best mentor hat I say, "It's nice to step back from good work and appreciate what you have accomplished." He steps back and agrees that it looks good.

Gesturing toward his feet, I point out, "You're standing on the onions in the first row."

"Oh, good lord," he says.

Next we head to one of the pig paddocks. The occupants have just made the trip to the processor, and the space needs cleaning up. Our first task is to roll up the braided strands of electric wire. To do the job we use a giant spool, much like an oversize fishing reel. And just like with the spool of fishing line, it is very easy to make a mess in quick order if you aren't paying close attention. The more fail-safe task is to unhook the electric wire from the plastic insulated posts. So I have the Kid start with that part of the project.

After a couple of minutes of watching him try to unhook the line from the first post, I get tired of tapping an impatient foot unnoticed.

"Here. You turn the crank. I'll unhook the wire. But be careful. Watch the spool and don't make a mess."

A few minutes later I look behind me. The Kid is merrily cranking away—a large bird's nest of tangled wire ballooning out of the spool.

"Hey, look what you are doing!" I bark.

"Oh, good lord."

Just before he leaves for the day, while we are putting away our tools, I lecture in my most teacherly voice: "You know, Kid, there are times out here when I might yell at you. Don't take it too hard. I just want us to get stuff done. And on those occasions when I get exasperated, you will know to either listen up or move faster. It is like with your parents; they yell at you because they care and want you to just pay attention. You know how that is. . . ."

He looks puzzled.

"My folks have never yelled at me."

"Oh, good lord," I say.

The prayer: Dear God, please cease punishing us with this plague. Scour the earth of these wicked creatures, if not now, then at least before blackberry season. So be it.

Seed ticks. For the experienced, those two words elicit immediate and involuntary scratching, perhaps even panic. It is midnight when I wake in my bed from a deep slumber, bolt upright, and make a mad dash to the bathroom with only the moonlight to guide my path. In the darkened corners of my sleeping brain an awareness of itching or biting in my nether regions has brought me sprinting toward the light. In the bathroom I drop my boxers and take a gander. It is not good. Dozens of red welts, each punctuated by a microscopic black spot, speckle my privates. The British food item of a similar name comes to mind as I give a horrified gasp. There is nothing to do but grab the tweezers and begin extricating the little buggers, one painful tweeze at a time.

Seed ticks, the larval stage of their full-size brethren, are born hungry. Before they can grow up to be big healthy ticks that menace man and beast, they start off needing a blooded host. When they hatch out they do so by the thousands, and if you are unlucky enough to brush against an emerging cluster, the larvae happily detach from their home—a blackberry bush or a low-lying tree branch—and attach to your body. Being shy and retiring creatures, they prefer and seek out the more private and sensitive tissues, taking multiple sampling bites along the way before burrowing in to feed.

Seed ticks are almost invisible, so the first sign of their presence is often that midnight wakeup call. Some years ago on an overnight at a primitive campsite, we received such a call: Nestled in our sleeping bags, an ouch, an itch, a fumbled grab for the flashlight, the evidence dotted both of our bodies. We looked at each other and nodded in horror, hastily rolled up our sleeping bags and packed away our tent, shouldered our backpacks, and hiked three miles under a full moon to the jeep. Then we drove, squirming, an hour and a half back home . . . where we immediately went to work tweezing the tiny blood suckers out of our skin.

Chiggers. They are a merit badge of spring and summer you never wanted to earn. I am five years old, proud of the three gallons of plump blackberries I have picked with my family. But later that evening, around my waistband, behind my knees and between my legs, the red bumps begin to appear, soon followed by horrible itching. I would rather claw the flesh off the bones than endure any more. Mom and Dad call us kids together, all in a common misery. One at a time we are brought into the den, inspected wearing only our birthday suits, then doused with rubbing alcohol and calamine.

The itching and scratching remain as a reminder, long after the culprits are gone, that the mighty are easily felled by the mity. For treating both chiggers and seed ticks, Southerners swear by the aptly named Chigarid, a smelly camphoric first marketed in the year 1963. I travel with a bottle in my shaving kit, for to be caught far away from home in the midst of an outbreak is to contemplate dark thoughts indeed, though for actual recovery time I'm reminded of the old saw about poison ivy: that it takes fourteen days with treatment or two weeks without.

Ah, the pleasures of blackberry season.

Sitting down with kith and kin at my father's ninety-first birthday, I am reminded that it is as children at the table that we learn how to live. The table of this celebration is weighed down with more than 150 pounds of crawfish and accompanying bags of spicy boiled corn and potatoes. A large platter of jambalaya made by a sister sits next to a plate for a vegan niece—a fake "hotdog" processed from who knows what. We variously stand and sit as we talk, laugh, and listen. Food, family, friends, and lots of conversation.

The role food plays on this day is the same role it played in my childhood (and still does in my adulthood), that of bringing people together. From the crawfish and crab boils to grand Sunday dinners and church picnics; from duck and chicken-and-sausage gumbos to BBQ and fried catfish, links of boudin, and platters of dirty rice; from running trotlines, fishing thirty miles out in the gulf, and hauling up shrimp nets or oyster tongs to shooting ducks and geese and harvesting deer, the end goal is always the same: food that you can share.

TV and computers were not part of my world as a child. No screen time, head down, eyes staring and glazed. You left the table only after you asked to be excused and were given permission. Weeknights were family dinners and catching up. Weekends and holidays were gatherings of the larger group of friends and family. And they were always set to the backdrop of food, meat, seafood, game, vegetables, and the ubiquitous dish of rice.

Sunday was the time for the big dinner of the week. It was frequently an occasion for serving up fish or seafood that we had caught—red snapper in butter and lemon, mackerel balls fried with a cornmeal dusting, platters of oysters, mounds of fried catfish, all accompanied by coils of the spicy local sausages warmed on the grill. The family would often be joined by guests, perhaps a couple of youth from Boys Town or a new minister and his family.

During one such dinner, with a new pastor from Oklahoma as our guest, we received a call from an elderly neighbor. Upon coming downstairs that fine spring morning, she found an alligator in her parlor. It had strolled in through an open door and made itself at home. My father used a ski rope to make a noose, slipped it over the beast's head, and dragged the gator back to the bayou, no doubt confirming in the new minister's mind his worst fears about where he had relocated his family.

Some Sundays after service we indulged ourselves at the Piccadilly. Dining at the small-town Southern restaurant was reminiscent of the Lyle Lovett song "Church." If your preacher became a bit long-winded, you might just find yourself waiting in line behind the First Baptists, or, God forbid, the Methodists.

From a kid's perspective Fridays were hopeful evenings. My parents were active in a supper club and a bridge club. Supper club in the house meant hovering near the kitchen to snag plates of Oysters Rockefeller fresh from the oven, bridge club loading up on shrimp broiled in butter and spices.

Annually, there were the church picnics, feasts of such epic proportions they required each of us to be heroes of the plate and fork. Whole tables were devoted to fried chicken and banana puddings, the memory of which would still be the Sirens' call onto the rocks of gluttony, except for the fact that underpinning all the food was fellowship.

So today, on our farm, with freezers full and gardens gathering steam, we ask the weekly question, what do we have to share and whom can we invite to join in the bounty—neighbors in the valley, friends from town or city, longer-distance guests?

Last night six friends helped us devour bowls of creamy grits topped with cooked-down collard greens and fried slices from a terrine of braised pork. We dined outside, sitting late into the evening as the full moon rose high in the sky. Good friends, conversation, and a bottle of elderberry mead helped us keep the faith with who we are as a people and the traditions we carry forward from childhood.

We have just pulled onto our road with the plan to meet friends at their nearby farm. As we round the curve below our property and pass the ancient falling-down Cook's Mill, we come upon a scene that is just unfolding. A car with a crumpled front end has pulled over and stopped in front of the mill. A woman is sitting in the driver's seat, red-faced and sobbing. A deer, gasping and unable to stand, lies on the other side of the road. We slow and turn around.

Cindy immediately approaches the driver, who had been on her way home from work when a deer appeared seemingly from nowhere and leapt in front of her older van. The woman is far more upset by the injured deer than by the damaged car. I approach the large doe on the side of the road. She holds her head upright. Blood trickles from her mouth. She is dying slowly. Somewhere, in the woods nearby, is a fawn. We can only hope that it was born early enough to be able to forage on its own now. We discuss what to do. Cindy stays with the distraught driver while the woman calls her husband, and I drive back up the road.

After first checking with a neighbor for a rifle, to no avail, I return with my own .30–30. It takes two shots to make sure the doe is dead—an act of mercy that is captured on a cell phone by a spectator in a Prius, for what purposes one can only speculate.

Once the van driver's husband arrives, we continue on to our scheduled appointment, the rifle behind the seat of the farm truck. At our friends' house we help them review plans for a cattle chute. We walk around afterward, admiring their growing gardens and newly built brick raised beds as we catch up on the day's news.

We pass the old mill on our return home. The damaged van is being loaded onto a tow truck. The deer is now hanging from a makeshift hoist on a tractor in our nearest neighbor's yard, already eviscerated and in the process of being skinned.

Back on the farm we tend the livestock, then sit on the back deck with our dinner and watch the night deepen over the ridge.

Ours is a particular kind of small farm. It's been called diverse, traditional, insignificant, wonderful, productive, inefficient, and a subdivision waiting to happen. We call it home, of course. On it we have miles of fencing, cattle (from time to time), sheep, pigs, chickens, ducks and geese, gardens, fruit and nut orchards, beehives, ponds, wine grapes, many species of birds, outbuildings, a sawmill, too many machines, pastures, and lots and lots of trees.

Over the decades our farm has increasingly seemed like an island. In a county where the small family farm model has historically held sway, the diverse home plot has been swept away by the incoming tide of the modern world. Spending time in hard, rewarding labor seems no longer to carry any attraction for most. The old-timers have died, and their farms have gone vacant or been taken over by occupants who are never seen except when their cars pull in or out of the drive.

The farm outbuildings have been torn down and burned, still-usable structures deemed unworthy of saving. The fencerows that once provided barriers for livestock and habitat for wildlife have been pulled up for putting greens, trampolines, and larger lawns. We knew in the past that if our livestock escaped, they would wander into the pasture of a neighbor, contained by their fences until we could retrieve them. Now they could amble unrestrained across untold acres and yards and roads.

Those who think this is a good thing, either a rewilding of nature or an extension of a suburban dream, would be wrong. It is merely an indication of a dying way of life, a giving way, a giving up on doing for yourself.

Yet there are hopeful signs in this changing landscape.

This year our longtime neighbor's daughter, now grown and with husband and two children, moved back to the farm where she was born. She and her family have begun to remake the mostly dormant property into an active hive of small-farm glory. Now, when I'm on a certain hill working, I hear the sounds of roosters crowing, goat kids and lambs bleating, a steer bawling, people on the land, talking, laughing, feeding, building, planting gardens and orchards—all telling the story of work and love for a place.

All are signs that this land will be more than just another address to house a Netflix account. And those neighbors are not alone. Some young friends of ours have recently bought their own small farm to try and achieve a similar dream of self-sufficing. They are now busy replacing old fencerows, emptying and repairing outbuildings, cutting cedars from the fields, raising chickens, and planting trees.

There are also the young people who come to volunteer on our farm from every point of the compass and globe. All want a more authentic life than that of an avatar in some digital dystopia of the corporations' making. All have plans of striking out for land with a hard stroke, creating an island life of their own in this modern sea. They seek not a life lived in isolation but one linked by an invisible thread to those who in the past shared the same dream, who share it now, and who will share it in the future.

6

None

Now is the office of the quiet hour, a time for either a short nap or a walk before returning to the task at hand. For this hour, on this day, the woods are my destination. I cross our pastures to travel a winding footpath through the oaks, maples, and poplars. Often my passage signals the start or the completion of a day of work. Today, I'll stop, pause, and reflect.

This small wood of twenty acres is divided by a steep ravine. Three off-shoots, broad church aisles of ridge land, converge on a private sanctuary in the heart of the forest, a natural presbytery for the unchurched. The time of day, the wind, the season, all influence where I stop and sit. I light a cigar and lean back against a tree and drift.

The light slants down, filtered, dropping in through high lancet windows of nature's cathedral. It falls onto and illuminates my pew, where the smoke lifts up through the leaves in an offering to the peace found in hushed observance.

The dogs bounce around like kids at a Sunday service, then pick up on the mood and settle near me. This is not a formal ceremony where members of the elite sit in designated and privileged seats. It is a come-as-you-are. Find a convenient rock, fallen tree, or flat ledge of land, and the observance begins when you are ready.

An hour of simply sitting brings to me a satisfying mental quiet in which thoughts eddy and swirl with the smoke along unexpected paths—a reverie softly interrupted by the distinctive devotional of a woodpecker, heard in its search for a communion grub, or the alarmed buck snort by the old man of the *woods as he catches a whiff of the dogs, his white-tailed flag flown, signaling if not surrender then at least a silent retreat up the central nave and out the back door.*

When my cigar is near its end, I stub it out on a nearby rock. The dogs are off chasing again, this time squirrels and the scattering scent of the vanished buck. A cloud obscures the light from the upper windows, and I, the remaining congregant, rise and start the journey home along a familiar and welcome path.

This late May morning, before the sunrise, the world is clothed in birds. They swoop, argue in the brush, sing, and chatter. They are everywhere in sound and flight.

Above my study, under the second-floor eave of the house, for the fifth year a pair of barn swallows rears its noisy brood. The parents forage nonstop. Upon their return they rest on a telephone wire forty feet out from the nest before diving in to drop a beetle into three waiting mouths.

Throughout the various barns and outbuildings of the farm countless other pairs are likewise nested. Together they provide one of my great delights as they follow the tractor, swooping in elegant patterns for unlucky and outmaneuvered insects.

At one end of the front porch a pair of house sparrows nests in a painted birdhouse Cindy created. On the other end a duo of cardinals has made a home in the crape myrtle, while farther out mockingbirds nest in the muscadine vines.

This season also brings us brown thrashers, bluebirds, blue jays, hummingbirds and their magnificently constructed nests in the apple trees, mourning doves among the crabapples, bobwhites calling from the overgrown fence line. And then there are the countless others that only Cindy recognizes: "Oh, my gosh! Out back, up by the blueberries, those are indigo buntings—the first ones I've ever seen!" "Look, out the window, quick! It's an American goldfinch . . . a pileated woodpecker . . . an Eastern kingbird. . . . Amazing! A Cooper's hawk. Too late. It's gone," she says, both sad and pleased for having witnessed its presence.

Each spring morning, after an hour or two of owning this time, my daily ritual ends. The sun pushes aside the songsters' trilling and chirping to take up its own dominion. In a sleight-of-hand the intensity from the early morning is diminished, as if the sun exercises some curious power, by illumination alone, over this sound, moving the birdsong to the background.

We receive a lot of visitors to our farm. Most are thoughtful and respectful of our time, appreciative of what we have to offer. We enjoy the showing and explaining of our routines. For many it is their first outing to any sort of farm. Some of them need guidelines on how to behave, so I put together this guide to the dos and don'ts of a visit:

1. Sturdy shoes don't have suede. High-heeled designer boots prancing calf-deep in pig muck, Italian loafers tiptoeing through the sheep poop, bare-toed Birks shuffling through clover smothered with bees gathering pollen—all have all been worn by ill-prepared guests. A working farm means manure, nails, and insects that sting. There's a good reason we warn you to wear sturdy footwear.

2. "Arrive at 10" is not simply a suggestion. When we ask that you be here at 10 a.m., we expect you to arrive at 10 a.m. Not 9 and not 11. And certainly not 2 p.m., when we are just lying down for a nap. Farm work is never-ending. We will be at it five minutes before you arrive and back at it five minutes after you leave. Agreeing to let you come to "see" the farm is, in our mind, a treat and a courtesy. Respect our time and watch the clock. Be aware too of the subtle signal to end the visit. When we say, "Better settle in and help us do some work," don't be surprised if we hand you a pitchfork when you don't take the hint.

3. Pets are accidents in waiting. Don't bring your dog. Yes, he is the light of your life. And of course everyone deserves to scratch his fluffy head. He is well-behaved, you have perfect control . . . until he sees his first chicken or his first flock of sheep. Or much worse, our varmint-killing farm dog catches sight of this unexpected intruder. Tears will ensue. Trust me.

4. Children, Part 1: Playing with electric fencing. Our farm contains miles of electric fencing. There's a reason it keeps cattle, sheep, and pigs in their respective places. We will point it out as you stroll the farm. Don't touch it or pee on it. Don't let your kids touch or pee on it. (Yes, that's your responsibility.) When your darling daughter reaches down and grabs a six-joule hot-wire, well, again, tears will ensue. Trust me.

5. Children, Part 2: Harassing, damaging, or killing livestock. When your son squeezes the baby chick so tightly he squishes it, there is a proper first response. No, it is not consoling the crying boy. It is placating the horrified farmer, whose future egg layer hangs limp from chubby fingers. It is he who deserves consolation, if not at least the offer of compensation.

6. Children, Part 3: Staring at screens. You thought getting the kids out of the house to see a farm was a great idea, right? We do too. That's why we must insist that they refrain from wasting their visit staring at a tablet or iPhone. Leave the digital devices in the car.

7. Gates work best when latched. There are dozens of gates on this farm, and they all serve the same purpose of keeping the livestock contained. Feel free to walk the farm, but do close the gates behind you. And, yes, closing means latching.

8. Don't call it a "hobby" farm. We understand, the farm is fun and its animals cute. But we work to make it pay for itself and support our basic needs. The term "hobby farm" is a slur to the working rural community.

9. These are not therapy animals, and this is not a petting zoo. Remember that we raise animals to be slaughtered and eaten or otherwise provide for our basic needs. While they are on our farm, they are treated with respect, that is, fed and housed and handled with care. They are not here to be cuddled or coddled; they are here to provide healthy protein and amazing taste to yours and our dinner plate. Admire them, even pet them under supervision. But keep the life cycle in perspective while visiting.

10. It's all fun and games until someone gets sucked into the baler. There are a million ways to be injured or even killed on a farm. This is not an OSHA-sanctioned environment. Keep a close watch on your youngsters and husbands. And that fancy scarf around your neck? It is a magnet for a PTO shaft. You really don't want to find out what that means.

11. You are welcome to buy something. We don't charge to visit (although some farms do). But if you need eggs, veggies, honey, beef, pork, lamb, chicken, or even lumber, we have all available to sell at different times.

12. Dinner is served. We are generous with our time, and, truly, we are glad to have you visit. Be respectful, show an interest, and ask questions. And, if invited, we hope you'll accept our offer to stay for dinner.

Timing is everything, so we are told. And that's what I tell myself as I head toward the livestock trailer this afternoon. I've been bushhogging four nearby sheep paddocks while waiting on a good friend to show up to help castrate three piglets—which, when I think on it, is the definition of "good friend": the person who will show up to help castrate.

Earlier, as I finished the third pasture and was on my way to the last, Cindy had appeared at the top of the hill. She waved, I waved, I pointed to where I was going next, then we both waved again. A rural semaphore, it's one of the first helpful skills you learn when you make your move to the country.

This fourth field, on a steep north-facing slope, creates more than its share of, shall we say, clenching moments. So, with eyes and grip fully focused on keeping the tractor from somersaulting down the hill, I let my mind ramble. It is the notion of domestic politics that is much on my mind as I bushhog. In the effort to bridge the divide and enhance civility, I have suggested that we once again get assistance with the castration.

Castrating pigs is an unpleasant task that this particular friend has long helped with, without complaint. Because, although Cindy and I get along most amicably overall . . . well, there are those times. One of those times, when the partisan divide is felt at its most keenly sharpened point, is when a man and a woman are separating young male pigs from that which the pigs most desire to keep. It is during these periodic operations that our dear friend agrees to play the role of agile wrangler, mighty holder, and domestic buffer.

Musing thus as I finish the last pasture, I catch sight of Cindy waving again. This time the semaphore says, "Get ye hence up the hill." Cresting the hill and cruising across the outer corral on the tractor, I spy both our good friend and his brother, also a friend, lounging at the gate with a bottle each of my best beer.

In my prolonged absence the deed has been done. Our good friend wrangled and confined; his brother held the snout (anyone who's ever heard a pig squeal quickly learns the importance of snout holding) while Cindy wielded the scalpel.

Which reminds me, yet again, that timing really is everything. And now you know all that you need to know regarding handling young pigs.

❦

Well, I thought that was all you needed to know, but . . .

One week ago this past Friday we backed our livestock trailer up to a chute leading into a series of pig paddocks in the woods. There we swung open the door, and three newly purchased weanling piglets fled from the trailer, through the chute, and into the largest, one-acre paddock. And almost as immediately they slipped through the fence on the far side, the one that has held 300-pound hogs and twenty-pound piglets alike, without escape, for nearly twenty years. Once through, they scurried to unbroken freedom in the woods and pastures beyond.

An anxious hour of fruitless searching later, we brought in the big guns. Within minutes our farm dog Becky had tracked them down in the tall grass framing the lane at the top of the woods. We then proceeded to herd the weanlings a good hundred yards, along two fence lines, and back through the chute. This time we steered them across the paddock from which they had initially escaped and into (we hoped) a more secure smaller paddock.

Having quickly hooked up an electric wire that runs around the base of the paddock, we retired to a well-earned rest. A couple of hours later we checked on our captives, only to discover that this time they had breached the fencing of the smaller enclosure. This time, fortunately, they had only migrated into the larger paddock (whose fence they had breached earlier), so we once again moved them back into the smaller paddock.

The issue was that at around ten pounds each, these piglets were smaller than the usual weanlings we bring home. The electric wire, at its normal eight inches above the ground, allowed the trio to limbo easily under the single strand of electric and then squirm through the grids of the woven wire fence. Thirty minutes of lowering the electric in critical areas, and we again high-fived ourselves and resumed our nonporcine activities. Outsmarting pigs is one of our everyday accomplishments.

Saturday morning dawned with clear skies and piglets in the paddock. Throughout the day we would look in on them periodically. The respite was short-lived. Sometime between our afternoon nap and coffee they had found a new exit strategy and took it. We looked high, we looked low. We looked in the woods and in the fields. We brought in Becky, drove the truck up and down the road, called "piggy-piggy," and notified neighbors . . . all to no avail.

According to custom, guests were arriving for Saturday evening dinner within the hour, and we still had food to prepare, so we abandoned looking temporarily. Nonetheless, on the guests' arrival a search party formed and renewed the hunt. But again, a thorough combing of the area yielded no piglets.

On Sunday, with a full work schedule to complete, we took time out for multiple searches in an ever-expanding grid. Still no luck. I opined that although we could keep looking, the three little pigs had more than likely already been eaten by coyotes, died from lack of water, or crossed the road and taken up life as river pirates on Paint Rock Creek. My naysaying was ignored, and I was enjoined to return cheerfully to our search party of two.

Monday was Labor Day, and it was a repeat of the day before: farm work, searches, no pigs. Around seven in the evening, just before sitting down to a nice dinner I had prepared, Cindy first did a quick check-in on Facebook to see if anyone in our community had spotted three porcine escapees, whereupon she discovered, sure enough, that a neighbor's son on Big Sandy Road, a mile away over two ridges, had posted finding three piglets and had confined them to a makeshift pen. Was anyone missing pigs? the youth's mother asked. Frantic messaging and calls tracked down a few facts. One, the post had been made at noon on Sunday, the day before. Two, the piglets had escaped the holding pen that same afternoon. Three, numerous other neighbors had seen the pigs on the edge of a wood near the road.

We rushed through dinner, then headed to Big Sandy, a road that wends through a small rural valley, like ours, of homes, gardens, chickens, and the occasional larger livestock. We began knocking on doors, yoo-hooing as we went so the residents would know someone was approaching. We handed out farm cards and told each household what we were looking for: three little pigs. Most everyone we spoke with had seen them at some point over the previous twenty-four hours.

How those tiny pigs had travelled the distance they did in such a short time we still don't know. But they seemed now to have taken up residence in an overgrown wooded area and adjoining side yard alongside the road. After chatting with the couple whose son had caught our wayward pigs the previous day (and finding out the husband's father had built our chimney twenty years back), then catching up even more, we returned home.

Tuesday Cindy drove over to Big Sandy in the morning, found the piglets in the same spot that others had seen them, fed and watered them, then returned home to discuss a capture strategy with me. Now the end of the saga, in retrospect, is somewhat anti-climactic considering that we expended an extraordinary amount of time in discussion and preparation that afternoon to retrieve our pigs.

During the day we continued to receive messages and calls alerting us to sightings, leading one to suspect that not much happens in that valley—which, to be fair to the residents of Big Sandy, is the same for our valley.

Finally, around five in the afternoon, we pulled out of our long driveway in the truck, armed with slatted livestock panels reinforced with attached wire (making them escape-proof), a crate, more feed, more water, and, knowing from firsthand experience that pigs are indeed fast learners, an understanding that we probably only had one shot at their capture.

Sure enough, there, alongside the road, next to the small wooded patch and adjoining side yard, were the three little pigs. We stopped at the neighbor's house to inform him we were going to set up a temporary fence in his yard. By now of course he already knew the whole saga of the piglets and quickly gave his blessing. At the woods' edge the pigs busily rooted around in the grass, while on the road's edge passersby who also were aware of the Great Pig Escape stopped, wanting to know if they could help. Thanking them, we waved each on down the road. This was a job we needed to finish ourselves.

After some hurried last-minute strategizing, we unloaded our panels, setting up a square that was open on one end. We placed a little feed and water in the pen. And then, seventy-two hours after escaping, with virtually no hesitation, the three little pigs walked into the enclosure, and we closed the fourth panel. Within minutes we had them in the crate, and, panels loaded back up, scarcely believing our good fortune, we headed toward home. The Great Pig Escape was over.

The walk-through gate into the inner corral is as good a spot as any for a morning contemplation. I lean against it, coffee cup in hand. The previous night's waxing crescent moon is safely abed below the western horizon. Our flock of pregnant ewes and unbred yearlings lies clustered before me, like small snow-covered hillocks dimly visible against the dark ground. A smell of lanolin and grassy poop rises from their warmth. It is 5:30.

The stars hide their light behind low scalloped clouds. To the north, above the river, the distant glow marks the location of the county seat of Kingston. Otherwise, except for a few security lights dotting the valley, our presence on this earth seems almost benign.

A few of the ewes begin to rise, defecating and urinating before taking their first morning step. Theirs is a routine that can make fertilizing the land remarkably easy for the organized farmer: Confine the flock at night in a small area of the field. Once the sheep have arisen and eliminated in the morning, let them out. Move the enclosure the next night. As I watch another sheep stand and relieve herself, I pledge to harness some of the collective energy.

On the wooden fence railing of the corral roost six Bourbon Red tom turkeys, all destined for Christmas tables. For now they have the run of the farm, and they exist harmoniously with the chickens, ducks, sheep, dogs, and cats. They do not, however, venture to explore the pig paddocks. Perhaps the hungry eyes of our fellow omnivores put the turkeys off from strolling too close. If so, then why do they not resist my occasional picking up and squeezing of their fleshy parts? Do they sense not my predatory intent?

I listen, holding my breath, as one of the hogs in the nearby paddock shifts its bulk against the back of the shed. Does this portend a structural deficiency that will result at any moment in a 250-pound escapee? I exhale. The building still stands, and the hog rolls over, resuming its slumber. Too soon the metal slapping of the automatic feeder lids will begin, and it will continue all day. Although the hogs have two acres of wilds to explore, these days, in the twilight of their lives, they prefer to spend most of their time at the dinner table. Indeed, our pigs have an obesity problem, but it's a problem we both embrace and encourage.

Beyond the corral to the north, just past the long rows of collards and peppers, the hoop-house is a ghostly presence in the dark these two weeks before Halloween. Inside is a thriving patch of sweet potatoes that I continue to nurture, holding off on harvest until just before the first frost—a date whose arrival is anyone's guess in this time of accelerating climate instability.

One of the roosters lets out a challenging crow behind me. Taking that as a signal, and with my coffee cup now empty, I turn to finish my early morning stroll, first past the ram lambs and the sleeping ducks, then on to the orchard and the grapevines, before circling back to the house and inside for breakfast.

I need to take a walk in the woods and see a box turtle blending artfully with fallen leaves, or, looking off the trail, spot a lion's mane fruiting on a dying oak. If it is early morning the deer will stand still, unnoticed until unnerved by my nearness, then explode into action, bounding in long strides before leaping the barbed wire fence in the middle of the woods at the base of the long ridge bordering the farm's eastern edge.

My steps will retrace the tread of my own camino, one that curves not across Spain but through the twenty-acre wood to the back pastures. It will be peacefully quiet, my steps unnoticed in the damp leaves. Little flurries in a hickory off to my left will reveal the presence of a squirrel, scampering muted by distance. It will pause as it detects my passing and call with a series of barks to all other of its kin within hearing. If I were there.

There, not here, where I'm staring out a window at two cars, two trucks, two tractors, facing a never-ending to-do list of late fall tasks.

Here, where all the conversations about ballot counts, when this or that investigation might be concluded, stock market fluctuations, Netflix releases, the demise of brick and mortar retail, wheel taxes, state taxes, food taxes, special status, unspecial status, working classes, elites, middle classes, football, basketball, baseball, iPhone updates (now and again this evening), new laptop, new, new, new, more, more, more—here, where we live and work, all this seems a grotesque sideshow to what this world has on offer.

If I could just crumple the to-do list for the day, put off butchering the ducks for customers, not thin the turnip greens in the hoop-house, not move the pigs to the woods, would I use the time well?

I need to take a walk to the top of the hill at midnight, smell the approaching winter, smile at the distant lights of a neighbor's farm, hear the sounds of our farm as the coyote passing along the fence line hears them; to crunch the frost underfoot, see the achingly clear sky and stars overhead; to clear the mind, open the heart and the soul to the majestic, reject the mundane of our meager achievements.

I need to take a walk.

It's six o'clock, long before sunrise, and I'm dressing in the dark, moving quietly so as not to wake Cindy. Downstairs two of the three dogs sleep inside at night. Max stays indoors because he'll bark at any and all random night noises if left outside. Our newest addition, Buster, a rat terrier, stays in a crate because he is still a puppy. He is already scratching at his kennel by the time I switch on a light.

I open the front door, and both dogs barrel out into the darkness. I follow and, stepping off the porch, all three of us relieve ourselves in the front yard, sharing in one of life's finer pleasures, because, it must be said, taking a whizz outside whenever and mostly wherever the urge strikes is one of the great joys of rural life.

I leave them to their morning rounds and go back inside to fix coffee. Once it's made and poured, I settle in with my mug and read a couple of essays in *The New Yorker*. Bill McKibben has written a well-crafted piece on climate chaos. But, in typical fashion he closes by burying the doom and gloom in a ridiculous bit of "here is what we can do." A little like being on the Titanic and, with the frigid North Atlantic lapping at your feet, having the bartender say, "Boys, the drinks are on the house." It may make you feel better, but it isn't going to change the way the day ends.

Footsteps sound on the floor overhead, and I hear the window blind in the bedroom being raised. "He's back!" Cindy calls down to me. "He" is the regal twelve-point buck warily making his way across the upper pasture. I get to the kitchen window in time to see him crest the hill and disappear just as the sun comes up, traveling southeast to northwest as he has most mornings since late summer.

Of course now it is hunting season, and his usual morning constitutional, if continued, will take him into the gunsights of the two nearest farmers, both avid deer hunters. Their hunting doesn't bother me, since I do plenty of butchering myself, but today must be the buck's lucky day. Our dogs catch sight, and their barks cause him to slow and reverse course. Good choice, sir. The guns stay silent.

I pour out some feed for the three dogs. Becky, our English shepherd sentinel, has made an appearance after a night patrolling the barnyard. Buster, true to his breed, is afflicted with early morning ADHD. He grabs a bite of kibble, runs off the porch to look at a leaf, runs back up the steps and takes another morsel, runs off the porch to look at some goose poop.

Meanwhile, Cindy or I must stand guard to keep the other dogs, who remain laser-focused on the untended bowl of chow even as they wolf down their own breakfast, from inhaling his rations.

A similar pattern repeats itself in the woods with the feeding of the six hogs. Each is worried that the other is going to get more food, even though I've placed it in six separate locations. In a rustic game akin to musical chairs, they individually circle from spot to spot, pausing long enough to displace another hog, who in turns moves to the next spot, where it displaces another hog, who. . . . And round and round they go, snatching quick bites on the run.

I finish my feeding chores, then spend time shoveling out the manure and bedding from the livestock trailer before returning to the house for breakfast. Cindy and I chat over oatmeal about our individual and collective to-do lists. Agreeing that weighing the market lambs will require both of our attention, we finish breakfast, then grab our coats and go to the barn.

'Tis an hour or two before midnight when, walking stick in my right hand, oil lamp in my left, and Becky at my side, I stroll out the back door for the somewhat traditional Christmas walk up the hill pasture, while Cindy stays behind in the warm house, the other two dogs curled at her feet.

Up the rise by the pawpaw trees and through the gates we pass before entering the wooded lane, where the lantern throws imaginative and ominous shadows. Becky stays close to me instead of choosing to explore the night. An owl hoots far away. The tires of a late-night pickup whir on the highway below; they go silent for moments as the truck rounds a bend, then their sound reemerges just below the farm before fading into the distance.

Nearby lights from the neighbors we still do not know filter through the trees. The man and woman have been here for a decade, but I hear tell that they are soon moving back to Miami. Having spurned ours and others' overtures to be neighborly, and apparently more comfortable as city dwellers, like salmon they now return to the stream that spawned them.

I turn the corner of the lane and begin climbing the hill pasture. The remnants of the late fall forages gather thick around my boots. I breathe heavier as I crest the ridge, and the full moon comes into view. Always an hour or two late to rise in these steeper wooded valleys, its light dwarfs the one I carry.

I stand for ten minutes staring at the familiar face, unable to turn my gaze—just me and Becky and the man in the moon on this cold Christmas Eve. Eventually he slips behind a sleeve of clouds, breaking the spell. I turn and face back to the west. Our farmhouse sits below, the windows beckoning with an inviting glow.

Off in the distance, on both the northern and southern horizons, blinks the red of a newly invasive species, a cell phone tower. Unwanted and unloved, it signals our fear of being alone.

I call for my dog, unnoticed at my feet until she rises and begins without prompting the journey down the hill. I trudge through the tangled grasses, back down the lane, through the gates, and into the house. "I'm here," I announce.

I lower the wick on the lantern, and the flame goes out. I unplug the lights on the Christmas tree, pour a nightcap, and ascend the stairs. A little later, before turning out the house lights, I ponder whether tomorrow will see the first lambs of the season. Many of our ewes are heavily pregnant. And, as often occurs, that most innocent of livestock is born on this farm around the twenty-fifth of December.

Life on the farm has always presented a comforting predictability. A seasonality of changes: winter's arrival of lambs, marketing of the hogs come spring and fall, the early spring budding of fruits and vines, planting of the first cabbage beginning in late February or early March.

We have built our farming practices around that predictability, erring on the side of caution as suits the natural conservatism of the farmer. We know that September and October are the driest months and that lime can then be spread safely on our hills, and we act accordingly. We have learned to carry over enough hay from the previous year to bed the animals during the cold months. We reserve stores of firewood; we leave pastures fallow. We plan two timetables for the garden's plant starts just in case one planting is lost to weather, disease, or pests. Virtually every decision we make is based on the recurrent rhythms that vary year to year, though always within a framework that is understood.

But now come the unpredictable droughts and deluges. The earth is changing right before our eyes, and we can no longer count on a time to every purpose. The changes cannot be ignored, yet there is only so much adaptability we can accommodate. True, as a small farm we're able to shift course more easily, even as the smaller boat turns quicker on its keel than the barge. But in times of extreme and erratic turbulence, a different direction does not guarantee entry into a safe harbor. The history of our species teaches us that lesson, and the older geological record hammers the message home with humility.

Friends and family express amazement at our farm's independence and productivity. Indeed, we do produce all of our meat, most of our vegetables, and some of our fruit, and we've done so for two decades. Yet this small diverse farm, like everything else on earth, is tied into a vast web of interlocking connections of history, climate, culture, politics, supply chains, and industrial growth. It is impossible to be otherwise. Each external connection impacts our decisions and limits us in ways we only pretend to fathom. Our independence and security are as illusory and elusive as a foothold in the barnyard slurry.

As a farmer I tend to think in terms of fragility. The newborn lamb, chick, and piglet all need nourishment, water, and warmth to survive and grow. Those are the universal requirements of life. Remove one of the three and a frailty is introduced into the equation, and death becomes the inevitable outcome. A few days past I entered the barn only to find a dead lamb, a two-week-old lamb that only half an hour earlier seemed to be flourishing, now unexplainably lifeless, now food for carrion. Fragility.

It is what that word "fragility" represents that most alarms me, keeps me awake at night. Its implications ripple out and shake history, culture, and that larger unknown, our sheltering climate (which more and more seems to have been just a window in time). These forces augur an ocean, churning up waves that threaten to toss us off our little moored raft into heaving waters, where we tread until we can tread no more.

We were chatting one day as we built a fence line, me and the Kid. This particular Kid had been working with me every Saturday for close to five years and was closing in on his twentieth birthday. I knew the broad outlines of his life and relations. So what he told me came as a surprise, when I asked after a grandmother who lived next door to his family. His response was something I've pondered many times in the intervening years.

He had never had a significant conversation with his grandmother: did not know how old she was, where she was born, who her people were. He had never stopped by just to sit with her, to talk, ask, listen. Neither of these two, in and out of one another's house and life for twenty years, had ever exercised the minimum of curiosity called for to learn about the other. Atoms floating together in the cosmos, yet neither magnetized by the familial connection.

I grew up amidst spoken volumes of family stories, an experience that is not at all unusual. Cindy comes from a similar background, as do most of my peers of a similar age. We all were surrounded by memory-keepers. And now I wondered, is that a tradition that is ending?

My aunt, soon to be ninety-nine, is by inclination, ability, and longevity a memory-keeper for my family. A woman who still recalls the names of and gifts from each person who gave her a wedding present in 1945 is someone to be respected. As important as the capacity to recall such ephemera of one's life are the ability and willingness to be a storyteller, to be the person who weaves the details of personal experience into a meaningful narrative that sheds light on class, history, family, and place.

The role of memory-keeper is as old as our race, but its status in these times is precarious. Our ongoing political project of individual liberty, supported by our technological self-absorption, has freed us from the connections of those who came before. The courtesies of community are now left to be redefined by an ever more ambitious globalism. The struggle of the modern has become one of repudiation of place and a need for constant reinvention. The result is that we no longer belong. We are left floating unmoored, selecting a story to tell that has been personalized for us by others, complete with a "who" we have decided to be in this moment, cut off from embarrassments of birth, childhood, and parentage, scrubbed clean of politically incorrect markers.

We have become too prideful of who we are as individuals, too ignorant in self-interest to want to understand, let alone embrace, the intricate web that defines us. In truth, we see no web. We pretend a text message is the same as a lunch with a friend. We believe a wave of the hand sufficient substitute for a face-to-face with a grandmother or grandfather, aunt or uncle, niece or nephew.

Even dinners and evenings sitting on a screened porch now leave no place for the elders to share their stories. The great floods. The first and second world wars. How my grandfather lost his business, farm, and fortune to the Depression yet still managed to support his family by taking work with the New Deal's Civilian Conservation Corps. Without those slow evenings I would have missed out on playing checkers with that same grandfather, missed out on learning how to lose the game and still win. I won, because, while he hooted with laughter and hollered "run piggy, run!" as he chased my last remaining piece around the board, he also told me stories of family—our heroes and our rascals—told me of his life, taught me who I was. Memory-keeping needs time, space, pacing, and even checkers to flourish. Most important, it needs love.

That we live in a segregated society, walled off from people of a different age and from our own past, is not new. But now, as our memory-keeper nears the end of life, few care to know her stories, or their own. A memory-keeper needs a listener. And a memory needs a caretaker, someone willing to take on the responsibility, accept the burden, to continue to tell who we were and still are. That role has become obsolete. It has been handed off to the faceless and unknowable, entrusted to server farms and social media, and we are left with the carefully curated life of the moment.

Now our living, breathing memory-keeper is no more. She is rebranded instead as a scrapbooking product sold at Walmart, the oral traditions of the millennia having been reduced to a cheap item bought, stored on a remote shelf, and eventually discarded. That is who we are now, what we have accepted.

In the morning of the first hour the room was without form, and void; and darkness was upon the face of the sleeping. And the farmer awoke and went downstairs in the dark and flipping the switch said, Let there be light. And seeing the light he said, This is not good, and turned it off, making the sacred bean drink in that dark, which was then separate from the light. Taking a sip he said that it was good, and he turned the light back on.

After staring without expression over a bowl of cereal for most of the second hour he rose and spread the previous night's waters on a convenient bush outside and called this irrigation.

He then walked among the gardens and diverted other waters, calling some "cistern-waters" and others "well-waters." And in so doing he nourished the plants called brassicas and the others he called weeds.

The porch light was still on, dividing the night from the day; and it was made diminished by the larger light rising in the east. The kitchen light, now aglow, showed the awakened presence of she who rules both night and day. And it was good that he was outside.

Now the fowl, that only fly with great awkwardness, were loosed from their coop. They were given two charges: pursue the small bothersome creatures that no one cares for and rapidly craft nourishing eggs. Then the lambs that bleat tirelessly continued to do so without letting up: and it was not good; so he commanded them to cease; and they did not, making the farmer reconsider his decision to release these creatures upon the land. This was the fifth hour, and already he tired from his labors.

Yet he continued, by taking pictures of his likeness and also that of she who rules the night and day, posting them to the Cloud. Laboring still more in this realm he "liked," "smiled," and "angry-faced" the remainder of this time to its completion. And he said, This is merely okay good and not really useful to my day or the many things that I ignore.

In the seventh hour he decided that this was enough, so he called to her, Let us lie down and take a short nap before we enjoy more of the re-freshing sacred bean drink. And they did, and it was a good use of their time. Whereupon they arose and piddled around for many hours doing this and that before they lay down yet again and withdrew into darkness.

And that was very good.

Like many, I grew up saying grace before the meal. In my house we sat down together for dinner or supper, then paused. A prayer was offered by a member of the family before all began to eat, the words always including a thanks for the food that was before us. No one ate before everyone was served and the blessing was said. Of course a nibble from the plate was fine. But it was not only a household offense but also a violation of cultural mores to grab a fork and dig in before each member was ready and grace had been said.

Blessing the food, saying a few words, is an ancient ritual. It crosses all religions and backgrounds; it is one of the most elemental of our sacra-ments. Acknowledgment to whatever creator or force one believes in seems one of our more beautiful and beneficial rites. An exercise of thanks for what is before us, of gratefulness for the bounty; patience in waiting until all have been served; humility in recognition that others may be doing without; and pleasure in the knowledge that there are family and guests, a community, with whom to share the food—all are rolled up in those few words said at the start of a meal.

Today, unless I am sitting down with people who share a common cultural or religious background, I find that offering thanks has become an awkward rite in both its recognition and its execution. To sit still and refrain from eating till all are served is a custom increasingly ignored. Witness adult men and women greedily shoveling food in their faces, plates already half empty, who then look up at a waiting table and say defensively, "Well, I'm not waiting!" It's a statement that neatly sums up the narcissistic spirit of our times.

Among a certain group of moderns the actual offering of a blessing or thanks now seems artificial, like passing around an artifact of carefully chipped flint, a relic of another age. Yet the sentiment lingers, even if manifested in a simple raising of glasses.

My religious friends and family can still roll out a beautiful and meaningful prayer at the drop of a hat, one that includes each of the four points of the ritual: thanks, patience, humility, and community. The words offered are still unencumbered by loss of faith or tradition. My own utterances, meanwhile, seem stilted, unpoetic, and rusted from ill-use and the lack of expectation from listening ears. Those spoken words of mine float about, against the crosscurrent, searching for a cadence and rhythm, searching for a home, trying to express humble gratitude for our rich existence on this planet.

7

Vespers

AT EVENSONG, I PULL up my chair into the bee-loud glade and sit down in the shade of a young oak. It is a mere child of fifteen years, with nearly two centuries of growth ahead. Yet, already sturdy and full, it provides a cooling shelter for myself and our small bee yard.

Storms build in the west as the sun, already hidden, prepares for departure, his work done. This is the office for the ending of the day, sung as a work chantey by humming bees finishing up their own day's labor. Laden like the stevedores of old, they return to their community one last time, corbiculae packed with pollen for the brood. Soon the daybridge will be pulled up in readiness for the night and her watchmen.

In the poultry yard nearby, the chickens join in chorus with the bees and begin the return to roost. They flutter up into the coop, where their elder aunts have already gone to bed. The roosters, giving a last challenge to the fading light, crow once more, then declare victory and retire from battle. In the lower fields the sheep still graze. Soon though, the dominant ewe will signal an end to the day. She will lead the flock in a doxology of contented bleats back to the barn, all readiness for rest and security. Vespers on the farm is a coming home.

Next to me is a small hive worked earlier in the day, a captured swarm from a friend and neighbor's apple orchard. Eleven days it has labored in building a new home with the old queen. We were prepared to find it weak, to merge it with a stronger hive. Yet the queen still lived, busy laying eggs, building brood, surrounded by her attendants. No, not yet a strong hive, but with luck, hard work, and the inevitable act of regicide, like the corn kings of *folklore, the colony will end the summer and fall strong enough to survive the next winter.*

I sit in idleness and rest as these last bees return from the field. I watch as they and their sisters gather on the landing board in tight-knit community. With news exchanged, plans made for the following day, they begin to go indoors.

Rising, I put my ear to one of the hives and listen to the hum of their evening song. It's a melody picked up throughout the farm. I pause and listen for the refrain, and then, as the poet says, I hear it in the deep heart's core.

I should be outside mowing the lawn. Claiming that the mercury is climbing is really not an excuse or a reality, for it is a perfect Saturday afternoon with highs in the mid-eighties and lowish for East Tennessee humidity. That the morning was productive—a gutter cleaning, the daily harvest of crowder peas, weed-eating around the day's rotation of trees, vines, bushes, and outbuildings—seems to matter not. Through the open window my mower's kin call gaily out to mine from up and down the valley, "Come out and play."

Slamming the window on their beckoning, I determine to focus my considerable energies on more fruitful projects. An hour later, a handful of computer chess game victories under my belt (all praise the Undo button!), I continue to wrestle with my work-avoidance and open the refrigerator.

A little snack to fortify my willpower for the afternoon is called for in this moment. Before me, in a dish gifted by my ancient aunt, lie salty duck legs buried in white glistening lard. Beautiful confit! (The result of another work-avoidance project tackled earlier in the week when I should have been completing yet another farm task or three.)

I reach past the various salads and grab a hunk of cheddar. In mere moments it is turned into a delicious shredded mound. A few simple steps more—a bowl, a small jar of pimentos, drained, then tossed with the cheese, freshly ground pepper and a sprinkle of salt, a healthy dollop of Blue Plate mayonnaise, a wooden spoon to mix and mash—and I'm done.

There are moments in life, genius moments, that strike us all. Ford had his assembly line and Edison his lightbulb. It is in these smallest breaks in the eternal flow that the gods hold their breath: "Will he???" With the DNA of generations of can-do pioneers coursing through my veins, I answer with a resounding "Yes!" I will take that hill and scatter the naysayers. Give me that ceramic of confit and be quick about it, sires!

With two slices of sourdough, a heap of pimento cheese on top and shredded duck confit on bottom, all assembled into one glorious sandwich, I stand on the porch, my masterpiece in one hand and a cold beer in the other and dare the world.

But wait. Fortune smiles on me this Saturday afternoon. Do I see gathering clouds? They do look like they could carry rain, might even, in time, develop into dangerous thunderstorms. Should I dash out and mow and risk certain death on the chance of being struck with lightning?

Nay, I head back inside, unwilling to hazard depriving future generations of these awesome insights.

You are welcome.

High in one of our pear trees are three golden fruits left behind during the harvest. Whether this salvation was achieved by living remotely or from neglect and laziness of the farmer it is difficult to say. But each sunset, until we have the right well-timed storm, they still shine before their fall.

In the working-class neighborhood of Knoxville where we lived years ago, we walked one fine autumn evening the four blocks to the Bill Meyer baseball stadium. We waved at our neighbor two doors away as he serenaded with a recorder on his broad front porch. Down another block and around the corner, two friends called out from their porch and asked where we were going. They then joined us, their two small children in tow, in our stroll to our destination: an evening of minor-league entertainment.

We paid the modest $4 fee and found a cluster of empty seats in the packed stands. The local team, the Knoxville Blue Jays, was playing the Carolina Mudcats. The left field wall was the century-old Standard Knitting Mill, where out of the windows during breaks the workers would lean to catch the game and a breeze and a smoke. We sat on the bleachers, beer in one hand and hotdog in the other, and chatted and cheered before walking back home.

The mill closed soon after, partially bulldozed into rubble, the remainder left derelict and waiting for the same. The workers and community dispersed to wherever they could find purchase on a new life. The stadium followed, as the owners chased the bigger tourist dollars in an adjoining county. The marriage of the friends who walked with us, fractures in the foundation already visible to all who cared to notice, also fell. And the friend who serenaded us from his porch died unexpectedly a few years after that night.

This past Friday, having landed at the airport from a trip, I drove to a nursing home to sit with my aunt. She had broken her hip the previous weekend. Holding her hand, I asked her to tell me a story. For out of nearly a century of living she has a repertoire of thousands, and like a skilled troubadour she can pull them out and launch into a telling that places you, roots you, in a world that has disappeared. Some of the changes are to be embraced, some bring on a crippling nostalgia for what was lost, and others merely mark the gulf between today's techno-world and the landscape of her birth.

I leaned in and she told me for not the first time of the big flood of 1940 in Crowley, Louisiana. For five days the city lay under water. My aunt's father's house, built high, remained dry. The house was opened to the women and children who lived in nearby flooded homes. Where the men stayed she never said. For days guests lived on the big wrap-around porch and throughout the first floor. The men pushed boats through the muddy waters each day to retrieve Red Cross food packages and bring them to the women who lived on the porch.

After an hour, tired from my own trip and anxious to be home, yet guilty to be departing, I left her lying in her bed. That evening I sat in the backyard to plan out my fall work on the farm. So much to do this season before the winter. A notepad in front of me, I prepared to make notes and wrote nothing down. I just stared at those three golden pears waiting patiently for the wind to take them home.

There is mist hanging low on the hill above the farm. It flows before sunrise in rivers among the tall grass. In the rose-colored light it presents a glistening dew and touches with grace each spiderweb, highlighting them in countless numbers.

Turning my gaze away for only minutes, I look back to find that it is already gone. It has receded now into the lower reaches of the valley, vanishing, as mysterious in its departing as in its arriving, revealing in its ebbing, in the high hay of the hill pasture, a doe and her spring fawn. Surprised as I am, she, naked to the growing light, is not. She bounds gracefully out of sight, followed by her offspring. Now left alone except for my dogs, who root through the scuppernong vines for opossums who left their own leaving until too late, I sit.

Gradually to my ears comes the faint thrum of traffic ten miles distant. It winds its way through the various valleys and over the slanting ridges. Motor life returns to a workday rhythm after the holiday, pulsing through the outlying blood vessels into the city, draining the countryside of purpose other than that of a traveler's inn, of sorts, for greed and accumulation.

Is this our fate, I wonder, a mere warehouse of life purposed toward temporary gain? To drive past lost meanings in the lay of the land, unable even to parse the text of an old dying fencerow, eddying like mist around an ancient barn in the hollow, before we retreat to some fluorescent cubicle to cross off our remaining days?

In this aging epoch of ours, is it too late to envision a return to something different? Is there a rite, an investiture in the holy office of simple labor, a smoking censer swinging high and low that would cleanse our mess with a restorative blessing, allowing us to stay, to work on and with the earth? Would any supplication now offered find a listening and sympathetic ear?

Does our lover even love us anymore? Spurned for so long, paved over and ignored, gouged and robbed, would she still have us? Even want us? Always we acted as the domestic abuser. Will our promises of changed behavior now be believed?

We should have known, could have read the marriage register held deep in the vaults, that she had dallied with five other lovers and outlived each. That record telling of her vast patience, written over four and a half billion years, could have taught the reader that even now she has already conspired with her next consort to bury us deep in the rock.

We are mists, vanishing.

It's been a homestead weekend on the farm: rendering fatback into lard, salting down pork bellies for bacon, harvesting crabapples and then making rosemary-crabapple jelly, all of it capped by watching a magnificent full moon rise over the hill pasture.

As I watch the moon emerge, I glimpse the shard of a boyhood memory. Sitting on the bank of Contraband Bayou, a mile back through the dark woods of the old Barbe property, I am ten years old and fishing for alligator gar around midnight, the light of another full moon laying out a path across the sluggish water.

The years between eight and twelve are the best for boys. It's a time when they are no longer kids (at least in their own eyes) and before the awkward teenage years of figuring out how to fit in. It's a time when they are just old enough to be gone all day during the summer and often out at night without occasioning a search party, when parents, glad to be shed of them, give them greater latitude to roam, and when any hints of what adulthood might entail are only lightning strikes over the horizon.

That the character of a boy's life depends on the locale and time frame as much as on his parents and family, I am fully aware. It also depends on his reading habits. For there is a vast literature for boys (or there was, before literary sanitizers came into general use) to guide him in the spirit of adventure.

That literature, as much as the era and place, steered the ways in which I lived my Louisiana youth. My free days were spent building forts, riding bikes across town on quiet streets, exploring the length and breadth of the bayou in a beat-up jon boat, running trotlines all night or fishing for bass all day—alas, guided by my books, filching my father's pipe tobacco and from an old pipe found in a ditch smoking it with my friends until the tears ran down our faces.

Tom Sawyer (he of the pipe instruction, among other wholesome activities) and other boyhood literary heroes loomed large in my imagination. Theirs were the templates for a well-lived life. I read scores of books during those years, and of them five were my bibles: *The Adventures of Tom Sawyer* (Mark Twain), *Rascal: A Memoir of a Better Era* (Sterling North), *Ice Falcon* (Rita Ritchie), *Rifles for Watie* (Harold Keith), and *My Side of the Mountain* (Jean Craighead George).

Survive being lost in a cave, and then attend your own funeral. Build a canvas canoe in your own living room. Befriend a raccoon. Stow away with Vikings and explore medieval Iceland. Serve on both sides in the Civil War. Fall in love with a Cherokee girl. Run away from the city and live in the Catskills. All the life lessons I imagined I needed were found in those pages.

Indeed, each has shaped me in ways that I cannot fully touch, conjuring the ghost of memory, of innocence, of adventure, of a boy, one that even now I glimpse from time to time, usually, often, in the light of a full moon rising over the farm.

Call me. I have stood with Ishmael on the piers that surround the city, with the other Manhattoes, staring seaward, more times than I can count. I have voyaged with him to Nantucket and signed the articles, met Queequeg and seen Captain Ahab. I have looked seaward and yearned to spot the great white whale. But, yea, long about page 275 and facing 500 more, I abandon the adventure and leave Melville to sail alone.

I love *Moby Dick* for the language and the story. Still, it remains after decades part of an exclusive shelf: books begun and begun again, ones that I would really like to finish but somehow never do; books distinguished from those begun and discarded as soon as the brain reaches an understanding as to their true worth(lessness), those for which Dorothy Parker reserved the ignominious fate, "This is a book that should not be tossed aside lightly. It should be thrown with great force." The latter category is vast, the former very select.

The books I am talking of are the "retries." A retry is not the book the reader picks up and continues reading after a fifteen-year interim, as in the case of, say, a history of the Spanish Inquisition or the fall of the Byzantine Empire. (Because, really, how many auto-da-fé cook-offs does one need to witness, how many early medieval emperors does one need to know?) The true retry calls upon the reader to go back to the beginning, the first page, the first "Call me Ishmael."

On the shelf of retries, just to the left of *Moby Dick*, sits *A Confederacy of Dunces*. It is a book I am contractually obligated by the Motherland to read to its end at least once before I die. To date, I have read, and reread, and reread, the foreword by fellow Louisianan Walker Percy, the description of how he discovered the brilliance of John Kennedy Toole's manuscript only after the mother of the writer, who had committed suicide, pressed it into Percy's hands so many times he could no longer refuse it. Yet I have never ventured more than halfway through the actual story. I have on at least a dozen occasions stood alongside Ignatius J. Reilly in front of the D. H. Holmes department store, where together we watch (he of the green hunting cap squashed on his fat head and I of the gray tweed flat cap), both of us judging the crowds for signs of bad taste. Inevitably, though, somewhere around page 185, Ignatius J. and I part company. The story is laid aside in a place where, fully intending on picking it back up later that day, the next, or the next week and finishing it, I never do.

Eventually I recognize the inevitable. I dust and then shelve Mr. Toole next to Messrs. Melville, Faulkner, García Márquez, Gogol. . . .

I'm making this confession now not because I expect it to shame me into actually completing these works, but rather because there is the hope and dream that it gives more than a little insight into why I never quite finish weeding my row of turnips, why I lay aside the hoe only to pick it up again a week later and start at the very, very familiar beginning.

Today we speak of destiny.

I may wish for a different role in life. But, alas, although the home phone seldom rings, when it does I always answer with some hesitation. Are we marked at birth for the roles we will play in this life? Do the gods gather up a handful of archetypal or character dust and randomly start slinging it about—a little leadership landing there, a bit of maternal instinct here, the jovial, the innocent, the hero, cast willy-nilly over the sleeping infants. Is that how it works, what it all comes down to in the end? Me, an Angel of Death for this valley?

It pains me to make this public admission, but when an animal needs to be dispatched, I get the call. It is not a job I seek, yet it comes to me more often than I wish.

The neighbors with a mortally injured lamb who can't bring themselves to pull the trigger call me. Dying deer on the side of the road? I get the call. Pet chicken gasping its last breaths? I'm the man, Brian the Neck Wringer. It can all get a bit depressing, this being the spine for, shall we call them "the Timid." I'd much prefer that they get on with the job themselves. But they can't, they won't. They call.

If you are going to eat meat (hell, if you are going to drive a car) you are going to have blood on your hands. My attitude, perhaps, has more than a strong whiff of the judgmental. But it is justified, certainly. Soon after I first met Cindy, a neighbor's Doberman got into her barnyard and savaged her sheep. After watching the neighbor hem and haw over killing the bloodied and dying animals, I reached for the .410 in his hands and did the deed myself. I hate to see an animal suffer or a hard decision postponed on account of spinelessness masquerading as compassion.

I hasten to say I'm not insensitive (right?). I chalk up my willingness to kill to a lifetime of gutting catfish caught on trotlines from the family pond, cleaning speckled trout and dolphinfish all night after a day of fishing on the gulf, butchering hundreds of chickens raised to put meat on the table. You carry out these unpleasantries if you eat. Or did, before the advent of mass man and consumerism distanced us from death, allowed us to believe that it is better for the immigrant, the low-waged, the lower class to do our dirty work, butcher our meat, butcher our enemies. Before we washed our hands. . . .

Oddly, and perhaps one reason Cindy and I have been together for so many years, is that she is called upon for the opposite function. If the Angel of Mercy is needed the phone also rings. When a mother goose got separated from her goslings, colleagues at work called Cindy to solve the problem. When a dog gets injured in the valley—bitten by a snake, shot by a neighbor, hit by a car—the call comes for Cindy. Where my toolbox contains an axe, rifle, and knife, hers includes clear-eyed compassion and skills honed over decades of caring for animals in her charge.

Hers is the more rewarding role to play. People approach and give her hugs years later for helping nurse a beloved pet or farm animal back to health. I, on the other hand, get the careful nod, averted eyes—wary, they seem, lest I discern a limp in their step and go for my shotgun.

The annual holiday gathering on the farm is an event notable for its complete lack of politics. Nary a divisive comment heard nor nasty post is tweeted. Progress. Even the field of plate-and-bottle debris is modest when compared to years past. Still, like a glacial moraine deposited across a Vermont landscape, the remains could last for eons, all depending on our energy level in the coming day.

The spread of food is pork-centered. Among the evening's meaty delights are mounds of home-cured ham (prosciutto); slices of ponce, a stuffed and smoked pork stomach; various salamis, some home-cured, some store-bought; prosciutto-wrapped dates and cream cheese; and a homemade potted ham (pâté). A tray of boudin goes forgotten in the refrigerator in the pre-party rush. There are also platters of cheese and cheese balls, relish trays, endless homemade dips, cookies enough to induce a diabetic coma for the entire valley, and, to provide the merest illusion of heart-healthy balance, raw veggies (albeit accompanied by the ubiquitous ranch dressing).

To wash down the massive amounts of food presented, our nearly forty guests imbibe a proportionally massive quantity of wine, beer, hot mulled cider, soft drinks. . . . (Fortunately, my gifts from a guest—two bottles of outstanding home-distilled products, one a grape brandy aged in French oak and the other a corn whiskey aged in American oak—survive the evening intact and undetected in their hiding place.)

Attending the gathering is a good mix of farmers and gardeners, bee-keepers, horse people and cattle people, small-farm and small-town people, rural and urban. Halfway through the evening a fellow farmer catches my eye across the room. Her arm extended and a grimace on her face, she twinkles her fingers as if searching for something. A mislaid lamb perhaps. An earnest group of listeners surrounds her, all nodding. "I've been there," I imagine them saying, but I can't hear anything over the din.

The beekeepers take over the kitchen at one point, confabbing, I suspect, over the latest method of treating varroa mites. Then again, it may simply be the homemade cinnamon ice cream one of them doles out parsimoniously that keeps the colony near. Or maybe it is their hive instinct that causes them to remain clustered on a cold East Tennessee evening.

In the front room our Charlie Brown Christmas tree is on display. A scraggly cedar cut from the farm, then dressed up with special ornaments acquired over the years, it anchors the corner next to the crowded deacon's bench. Underneath the tree, among assorted presents, are jars of my freshly rendered lard, gifts to go home with our guests. Each jar sports a label designed by Cindy with the tagline "Good lard, it's tasty!"

The evening comes to a close past our usual bedtime, but not before a late-night trek en masse to the hoop-house for bouquets of turnip greens for the deserving. We do an initial tidying and retire upstairs to read for a while before enjoying a well-earned rest. I dream of a breakfast of fresh scones with double cream and lemon curd left for us by a friend and sleep soundly.

Like fat-bellied ships heavily laden with riches, our nineteen ewes lie uncomfortably at anchor, waiting to be offloaded. Lambing season began on Wednesday morning with a fine set of twins born to one of a small group of related ewes who possess a nervous eye and a high-stepping skittishness. In a herd of cattle such cows are dangerously overprotective and prone to charging. In a flock of sheep, such ewes, with their stomping and scattering, are merely an annoyance.

Taking turns, one of us around ten at night, another after midnight, again at three, and then between the hours of five and six, we walk softly amidst the flock where they lie. Out in the hay barn paddock, among logs lined up to be cut on the sawmill, we play the light over the tranquil sea. We look for new lambs and for bulging ewes standing separate from the flock. And we watch for the ones in distress and needing a helping hand. Thankfully, we are seldom called upon to assist.

It's three o'clock on Thursday morning. I step out onto the front porch to find the temperature unseasonably warm, with a near-full moon and clear skies. No light is needed as I enter the paddock and move gingerly through the mass of bedded ewes. These are the times when I am giddy with the love of farming.

As I walk I think of my favorite old neighbor, now gone, telling me two decades ago of his love for walking the hilly pastures among his dairy herd on a moonlit night. I have created my own path among the cattle and sheep. The wonderful earthy smell rising from the resting bodies, the sounds of deep breathing that signify all is well—they strike a soul-satisfying note in the husband.

On this night, too, all is well. I spend thirty minutes with the ewes and find myself reluctant to return to the house. Even back inside I toy with staying up, putting on the coffee, sitting quietly and reading. But I return to bed and sleep a couple more hours before getting back up and repeating the trip as the moon sets in the west.

Saturday morning I rise around five, having slept through my middle-of-the-night check on our charges and not knowing whether Cindy has ventured out into the balmy night. Storms are building in the distance, and change will soon be at hand.

I make coffee and dress. In the paddock I count lambs, shining my light over the ewes. One ewe lies at the edge of the flock. I come near, and she stands to allow a pair of snow-white newborns to suckle. They look strong and healthy, so I leave them to do what is natural and walk on. In the shelter of the hay barn's overhang is another ewe. She is also lying down, and beside her is a singleton. But unlike the twins, this lamb is positioned on its side, at an unusual angle, curled, but with the head stretched out. I touch it and find its coat still warm and damp with afterbirth, its tongue distended, its head already cold in death.

I rub it vigorously without either joy or hope. My sad expectations met, I leave the lamb on the ground next to its mother. She continues to lick the still body as if she might will a better outcome. We bury the newborn later in the morning. Even as the day merges into evening, the ewe continues to call for her lost lamb, breaking even the stoniest of hearts.

A newborn's death surrounded by so much new life is the essence of our work on the farm. We raise these animals for slaughter, for the table; we joke that sheep are born looking for ways to die. Yet there is always real grief at loss, especially that faltering misstep at birth.

The next morning I take another three o'clock walk among the sheep. The severe storms of the day and evening before have passed, leaving behind a clear moon and starlit skies to light my steps. All is well as I find two more sets of twins just born, unfaltering, into this world.

This life is not what was expected when first I took up farming. Even today it is hard to conjure the farmer I envisioned two decades ago. No doubt he was tweed-clad, leaning on a walking stick as he surveyed a vast fat and sassy flock of sheep. And, in truth, I have been that man, played that role, an East Tennessee member of an imaginary minor gentry. But more often than not I have played the fool in service to the foolish. And so it was to be on this day I shall describe.

Lambing season brings a level of noise that is hard to convey and even harder to endure. A bucket gets rattled fifty yards away, and a mob of ewes begins bawling in hopes that the farmer has gotten the feeding time wrong. The lambs pick up the chorus. And when the lambs begin bawling, the ewes turn their attention from the din of the feed bucket and begin calling their babies, all at once, who all respond, all at once. The only sane way to handle the chaos, which restarts every half-hour, is to try desperately to shut it out.

All of which is to point out that it was hardly my fault that I ignored a bleating lamb for more than four hours. I was working in my study that morning, tuning out the periodic bleat-in-unison and along with it the small, plaintive call of a lamb. Using the skills of not listening I've honed over thirty-five-plus years of domestic bliss, I focused instead on the tasks at hand, all the while meaning at some point to check on the annoying background noise. At lunchtime I ran some errands before returning home and taking a short nap. The bleat continued, I noted, and I filed my good intentions away to the back of my brain.

The back of the brain is where we store hard-to-retrieve items like "Don't forget to pick up some toilet paper in town" and "Wash that grease off your hands before using the yellow towels" and "I should probably be a good farmer and check on my livestock before doing anything else." But, and I'm paraphrasing here, the road to hell passes through to the back of the brain.

Another half-hour went by before I awoke refreshed and listened to the unrelenting rain (six inches in twenty-four hours, to be precise) falling on the tin roof for a few minutes more . . . and, finally, recalled the lamb's incessant bawl. That's when I went downstairs and pulled on my rain slicker, my battered fedora, and my Wellingtons and sloshed out to the barnyard.

The flock peered out from the hay barn, where having knocked over the carefully erected fence panels they were busily making a mess of my neatly stacked hay bales.

Over the ever-present din I could hear one tiny voice coming from somewhere else. Sure enough, looking for yet another way to die, wedged halfway across the dam of the nearest pond and standing in water up to its belly was a lamb. Apparently it had taken a wrong turn in the hill pasture and got separated from the flock. Doing what all good little lambs do, it panicked, tried to take a shortcut to the barn, and got trapped between a thorny wild rose in front and briars behind, the steep wall of the dam above and the three-foot-deep water below. A woven wire fence across the dam prevented the simple solution of my reaching down and pulling it to safety. My attempt to wade into the pond ended when the water level reached the top of my Wellingtons mere feet from shore.

Slosh, slosh, slosh back to the hay barn I went, ignoring the greedy sheep who were ignoring their distressed comrade while stuffing their faces on precious hay. I took down one of the kayaks from where they hung barnside, grabbing the smallest because it was lighter and easier to haul back to the pond. Only when I had squeezed my six-foot-two frame onto the six-foot craft did I wish I'd chosen the larger.

Kayaks are nifty vessels. They are light and maneuverable, but they are also prone to tipping their contents into cold water. I kicked off from the bank and sat perched atop the boat, an overladen barge ready to offload its cargo at any second. A few strokes of the paddle brought me across the pond to within two arms' lengths of the lamb—who about that time decided to move farther under the protection of the wild rose bush.

There I teetered on the narrow vessel. Above me in surround sound, on the bank and lining the dam, forty ewes and lambs had gathered. They watched intently my every move, voicing with enthusiastic bleats a wall of noise that would put to shame the lustiest cries at a gladiator game.

Sensing my moment I lunged, I missed, and the lamb squeezed even farther under the thorns of the rose bush and away from my grasping hands. The tipping and tilting kayak, meanwhile, had taken on a bucket's worth of cold March water, which now sloshed around my ankles. For the moment, I decided against a shotgun option to end the standoff; that would have entailed a cowardly retreat to the mucky bank and then house, 400 yards and several gates away.

Instead, I made what in all honesty was to be my last heroic lunge through the brambles. This time, having endured an armful of undeserved scratches and voiced unspeakable oaths, I was just able to grab the damn sodden wee beastie by the leg and hoist it into the kayak.

The lamb bucked and twisted, but I clung to the woolly ingrate with one hand and paddled frantically with the other, the featherweight boat lurching this way and that. It was only with much mutual surprise that we finally made it across the pond and drifted onto the far bank.

The onlooking sheep had long since lost interest in the spectacle and returned to the hay barn. The lamb and I exited the kayak, and both of us stood and shook ourselves off. The wayward babe then ran, bawling, to find its mother, unscathed from the ordeal. The ewe's maternal instinct suddenly kicked in, and she ran to greet her child, then the two rejoined the general mayhem in the barn. I left them to it as another carefully stacked round bale was being demolished . . . and once in the house went directly to the freezer and took out four lamb chops to thaw for dinner.

I walk with determination from the house, past the barn and chicken coop and into the hoop-house, with the sole goal of catching a rabbit munching on my tender cole crop transplants. Sunrise is still an hour or more away, and the light is just enough to see that while the rabbits had been having their way (again), none are visible and within blasting distance of my shotgun.

Come high summer I may take a live-and-let-live attitude toward the cute little rodents. At a time when we are deep in the largesse of a bountiful garden, I can afford a bit of noblesse oblige. But in these first days of spring, a sacrificial rabbit is the only deal on offer. There are only so many veggies to go around, and I'm not willing to share, unless the rabbits do the same.

Earlier in the week we spent a couple of hours castrating a dozen ram lambs. We left another two intact, both large singletons, that showed remarkable growth. We will graze them through the summer with Joey, the big boss ram, and see how they shape up for possible use in fall breeding. This morning, beyond the far open door of the hoop-house, past the nibbled kale, the ewes and their lambs lie at rest, scattered across the corral. Quiet for once, they seem at peace with the morning. I know this will change. For now, though, I simply take enjoyment in watching them.

I turn after a few minutes to walk back to the house. Passing the barn I glance inside to see how our neighbor's project is coming. He is enclosing for us a ten-by-sixteen-foot storage room with a low ramp to house equipment and tools. Anyone with experience around barns knows how dusty they quickly become. After twenty years with the need, we are finally moving forward with the construction. The flooring is down and the framed-in walls up. Standing on the floor, I give a jump and find it firm.

Back outside I approach our three beehives. A steady thrum of activity is audible from a foot away. The globally mandated Covid downtime allowed me the opportunity to act as Cindy's beekeeping assistant a couple of times this past week, lending muscle to her intelligent care of the hives. Two days ago she completed a split (a form of swarm intervention), creating a new hive, while I relaxed nearby in the shade and drank a beer with drop-in friends. Now, in the early hours, I listen as the newly split hive hums contentedly.

Before going to the house, I stop back by the barn and cast a nasty look at the lawnmower. Yesterday I gave it a start for its inaugural cutting. Only after pulling the cord and grimacing as it idled much too slowly did I realize that I had forgotten to replace the spring on the governor last fall. It was a simple enough fix, which raises the question, why wasn't it taken care of six months ago? That is one of those eternal questions I ask myself. The response is that it is all too easy to put aside a repair and move on to another task. The second-best response is to fix it on the spot. So, yesterday, that is what I prepared to do. Without thinking, I released the throttle to stop the engine. I then reached down to turn the mower on its side to repair the missing spring. It was at that exact moment that my pain receptors notified my brain that the blade was still spinning.

Thirty minutes later, after bandaging my bruised and bleeding fingers (each mercifully still attached), Cindy went back to her small tractor and continued mowing around the barns and outbuildings—but not before sagely suggesting that I call it quits and instead self-isolate in the backyard with a beer. I did, vowing to maintain proper social distancing from the mower, at least until next week.

The sun rarely shines these days. The rains have set into our valley and don't know when to stop. Farming chores are carried out in quick bursts between downpours, and plantings are postponed until a day when the storms finally subside.

Something doesn't fit, like a key in the wrong lock. We oversow our pastures with cool-weather grasses and legumes, then plan for another round next month with warm-weather seeds. We wait for the sun to assist, but it demurs. The sheep stand at the barn door and look longingly at pastures denied. "Have patience, girls. The sun surely will come out someday," I tell them. They are not to be convinced with words.

I call some of our elderly neighbors to ask if we can get them anything at the grocery store, hoping to spare them the risk of Covid exposure. It has been, shamefully, a year since I last spoke with most. "My wife has been diagnosed with lung cancer," I am told by one, deepening my embarrassment and my fear for them. Cindy speaks with another couple, both in poor health. They are good neighbors who share a fence line. The man, a farmer who has never stinted on labor or advice for these past twenty years, is in his eighties. Cindy promises to visit and extends the same offer of groceries and other supplies.

I use FaceTime with my aunt. She will turn a hundred come July. She looks at the phone, at my face, turns to her caregiver and says, "Isn't it amazing?" Locked down in assisted living, she recalls the stories told to her of the 1918–19 flu pandemic. She understands. My father will celebrate his ninety-third birthday in a few weeks in reduced company; our annual crawfish boil, with the extended family in happy attendance, has been canceled until better times. I wonder, is reducing the risk really worth the sacrifice of touch and companionship?

Friends and colleagues are furloughed, giving me more time than I have had in years to farm and garden. Yet what should bring me joy merely makes me sad. There is hope, I know. But there is also an awareness that what has been squandered lies rusted on the ground and what has been shattered doesn't fit back together the same, if at all.

These are the cycles of history. Just as our generations no longer grieve at past horrors recorded in seldom-read books, in a hundred years hence only the bore or the academic will find interest in this age when our little dramas all fell away.

Still, with hope, we wait for seeds to sprout.

"History may not repeat itself, but it does rhyme."—*Mark Twain*

Our phone has been ringing off the hook again, and we are glad. But now I have some questions without ready answers.

In the wake of the 2008 Great Recession small farms did, if not actually thrive, at least fare better than they had for some years before. The population, already primed by Michael Pollan and *Food, Inc.*, deluged us with requests for sides of pork, quarters of beef, whole lamb, chicken, eggs, and produce. We hosted workshops on foraging mushrooms and raising hogs. We conducted classes on butchering chickens in which we had real estate agents lined up next to home-school moms, waiting apprehensively to wield a knife on a live bird. The job loss, the foreclosures, the crash of the banks—the societal disruption was such that virtually everyone feared being relegated to living a quasi-medieval life before that year or the next was out. For the first time in a long time people thought and acted local. That lasted for a few years.

What does the future post-Covid world hold for the small farm? Where will it fit into the economy, or more to the point, which economy will it fit into? Because, like history, an economy ain't static.

A recent article mentioned offhandedly that Americans eat 75 percent of their vegetables at restaurants. That stat shows the outsized impact of our consumer economy on what used to be a family or communal experience, whether it be sitting down to shell beans or to break bread. We have, in one generation or two, outsourced the love and care of food preparation and delivery to businesses. (Which raises the question of what the heck is in those veggieless home-cooked meals.)

Dan Barber, in his book *The Third Plate*, spent several hundred pages eloquently reimagining the dinner plate of the future at his elegant Blue Hill restaurant. One of the questions that still rattles around in my brain is, does a future knocked from its pedestal by global catastrophe (pandemic, climate change, collapsing resources) really allow for high-end restaurants or, indeed, for restaurants at the scale we have today?

A local producer (or as it is now fashionable to say, "maker") remains only a twee option in the global consumer economy. When the customer sees "local" as a consumer's choice—"I bought some lovely pork chops from Winged Elm Farm, honey. Run to Costco and pick up the rest of the meal's ingredients"—Costco (or another big box grocery) will always be the default. While that "choice" continues, most small farms will be but a rhetorical flourish for the politician, the food writer, and the conversationalist at the restaurant dinner table, a footnote on the farm-to-table menu that proudly announces sourcing local ingredients "when available." In short, the small farm is still marginalized, honored in the breach, not as an essential part of the larger market.

Small-farm culture simply is not relevant in large-scale capitalist or command economies. It exists in the margins of most economic models; it endures, in moments of time, as a particular cycle of history expands or contracts. The census used to have a category for the "self-sufficing farm," an entity that produced the majority of a family's needs and bartered in a primarily cashless economy for the remainder. That model, while not so sexy to policy planners, politicians, or, frankly, you and me, is closer to how most small farms have existed across the centuries, across the continents. Perhaps the small farm thrives when there is minimal choice?

One day next month or next year this particular crisis will pass, no doubt. But it has left exposed the limits of global supply chains. It is encouraging that those limits are now being questioned. But I don't think that good questions or good answers will change our trajectory as a species. Just as likely is that the planet will make the choices for us. Then the question becomes not, where does the small farm fit into the economy? but instead, how does the larger population learn to live a life of reduced choices?

Older farmers in this valley recall that when they were growing up, an egg man used to come around twice a week to collect eggs. He would take them to sell to the family-owned grocery store in the nearest town. He provided some much-needed cash for the farms to buy what they did not themselves produce.

Maybe that is the best outcome we might hope for: when the clearest sign that we have launched ourselves on a new and better course is that one fine spring day, as we are hoeing in our gardens, we once again hear the sound of the egg man coming up the lane.

❊

Nothing is duller than a prepackaged seed packet. What started in January with the hopeful perusal of vegetable catalogs ends in February with the arrival of parsimonious clutches of lonely seeds, each variety sprinkled into the bottom of a small envelope. Like the childhood prize in a box of Cracker Jacks, the reward is always less than one had hoped for.

It was usually in late March, in coastal Louisiana, that my brother and I would accompany our father to the local hardware store to buy our annual garden seed. The store was an old-fashioned place. Galvanized washtubs and spring-jawed animal traps hung in jumbled confusion over open bins of seed. The bins were mounted on boards and sawhorses, side by side, and filled the entire middle aisle.

The seed choices seemed unlimited: Beans of every color and pattern. Pole beans, bush beans, butter beans, crowders, and cowpeas. Kentucky Wonder, Grandma Rose's Italian, Rattlesnake. Fungicide-treated corn dyed shocking pink and labeled with quaint names like Country Gentleman and Golden Bantam. Collards and turnips, and, of course, mustard greens, the lovely regional belle courted by all.

At each bin awaited a scoop and a stack of brown paper bags in small, medium, and "I'm going to feed the world" large. Even today I can conjure the sound and feel of running my hands through the bins, allowing handfuls of pole beans or okra seeds to cascade through my fingers.

Preassembled seed packets are, at best, for the social isolate. They are the paint swatches to the painted wall, a meager sample of a promised result. They are the anti-community.

Yes, yes, yes, I buy seeds in packages. And yes, commercial seeds have been mailed out for at least a century and a half. And yes, the commerce of the mailbox differs but in kind from the commerce of the bricks-and-mortar. Except, except (and unless you have had the pleasure of buying seeds in the old-fashioned way, you cannot understand this), when your father tells you to grab a scoop and get a half-pound of Romano-type bush beans, something tangible happens. You have become part of a membership.

When you carry your paper sack up to the front of the small hardware store and place it on the scarred wooden counter next to the seeds your father and brother have selected, and the owner says, "Good afternoon, Mr. Bill. Who we do have here?" and your father replies, "These are my sons, Keith and Brian"—well, that is not just a packet of seeds arriving in the mail or bought off the rack at the big box. It's not just a purchase, in fact. It is the seed of something more, something needed, something that provides for so much more than a mundane meal.

I crest the ridge and open the door to the truck and get out to close the gate. I stand there for a minute watering the ground as I watch the clouds building in the west. My shirt is wet through with sweat and sticks to me, now suddenly cool on this sweltering afternoon. The hayfield around me neatly cut, the farmyard below in order, I'm put in just the right frame of mind as I get back in, shut the door, and restart the engine. I have a big grin on my face as the truck bumps across the field in time to Marty Stuart's "Hillbilly Rock" blasting out the speakers. Damn the soaring global temperatures and depleting fossil fuels! I do love a farm truck.

Out of the pasture, past the house, I just keep going. The tank full of gas, a couple of chainsaws rattling around in the bed alongside a couple of salt blocks and a square bale of hay, I stop long enough at the gate to call Max and Buster. They jump in the truck cab, and we turn out onto the road.

We tool past the old Cook's Mill right as Marty launches into "Now That's Country." I'm not going anywhere; it's just me and two dogs enjoying a hot summer day. We hook a left onto Johnson Valley and poke along, taking in the sights. The windows are down, and Max sticks his massive head out far enough that I'm afraid a stray branch might lop it off. Buster sits between us like a kid with his parents, staring straight ahead. Both are drooling with the excitement. Apparently we all agree: the destination isn't important. And anyway, in the long and lonely years since Galyon's community store closed, there isn't anywhere close by to stop, even if for no more than an ice cream sandwich.

A farm truck shouldn't be a pretty truck, tricked out with bells and whistles and buffed to perfection. Frankly, it helps if it is dirty and a bit beat up, particularly if it is going to inspire the pure bliss of a summer afternoon's aimless ramble. It also doesn't necessarily have to be old to have character. As Indiana Jones says, "It ain't the years; it's the mileage." My farm truck smells of sweat and ground-in dirt and pig and sheep manure, and the ripped cloth seats are covered in dog hair—a mirror of sorts to the farmer and, as such, an ideal mode of transport for which no shower is required before entry. It has a half-dozen CDs crammed into the console, with a music selection curated for the back roads, mainly country, bluegrass, and Southern rock. Because, let's be honest: somehow Miles Davis just doesn't cut it for a hands-keeping-rhythm-on-the-steering-wheel good time.

We turn onto Raby Town Road, and Marty and Randy Travis begin a duet of "This One's Gonna Hurt You (For a Long, Long Time)." The dogs and I both get into the act and start vocalizing our own rendition of the song. We rumble past the Cedar Fork cemetery, extending a tip of the hat to my favorite neighbor buried here, before making the few turns that put us onto Lynn Road.

Man, the three of us are over the moon, and I've picked up speed, and I'm driving faster than is reasonable on the one-and-a-half-lane road. Marty sings us back out to Stockton Valley with "Western Girls." Max has given up drooling out the passenger window and has pushed little Buster out of the way and has climbed into my lap, all ninety pounds of him. I'm laughing like a maniac as he tries to lick my face, and I'm trying not to run off the road. Another five minutes and we pull back onto the farm's gravel drive and straight up the hill to the barn, where the dogs dive out the open door and I head inside for a much-needed shower.

Dear Nephew,

Congratulations on your desire to purchase a farm. It is a great move, and you are the right age to make a go of it. I'm going to give you some advice, lessons I learned from a starting point of ignorance. Listen and learn.

- *Farming attracts fads like bare legs attract chiggers.* There is No Magic Next New Thing to succeed. Go old school and care for your land, animals, and family; work hard and be frugal.

- *Ground yourself.* Read anything by Wendell Berry, Gene Logsdon, and Joel Salatin.

- *Arm yourself, reasonably.* Shotgun, hunting rifle, .22 caliber—all have a place on the farm. You don't need anything else unless you are preparing for your own Ruby Ridge, in which case you should rethink your reasons for wanting to farm.

- *Move to the country not to get away from people but to get closer to them.* Prepare to have neighbors on whom you can rely, not just wave at.

- *In that vein, start by helping others.* Notify the nearby farmer when his cattle are heading down the road; better still, ask if you can assist in putting them back in the field. Volunteer to lend a hand in butchering the neighbor's deer or chickens. Join the old man across the lane when he's picking up square bales.

- *If you attend church, pick one that is part of the community, small enough that you are known.*

- *Buy a pickup truck, preferably a four-wheel drive.* There's no need to get a farm truck duded out with heated seats and sunroof. There's also no need for a livestock trailer at first; just rent one at your nearest farmers co-op.

- *Get an older tractor that you can repair and that has the power you need.* You have the mechanical skills to keep it in good condition. An American-made thirty-five to forty-five horsepower from the sixties or seventies should serve you well.

- *Raise what you like to eat.* That applies to vegetables, fruit, and livestock. If celeriac, aronia berries, and emu meat are your go-to ingredients for an average weekday dinner, then dive right in and raise them. If not, then make a new list.

- *That said, one of the great joys of having a farm is to experiment with what you grow.* Just cover the basics first, and consider these variables in your decisions: What do others in your area grow or raise? What does the land support? You wouldn't invest in an olive grove in Minnesota, and you wouldn't farm salmon in Louisiana.

- *Plant fruit, nut, and shade trees as soon as you can afford it.* Sow cover crops or oversow grass seed in your pastures, then fence, fence, and fence some more.

- *Share your overabundant harvest.* If you're wanting to sell your bounty to others, think about this: Where is your market? It's liberating to live three hours from the nearest large city, but who will buy what you produce? Begin putting together a list of outlets for possible customers.

- *Treat what you raise with respect and cook it with love.* I know you are of sound Louisiana stock, but you also have been culinarily disadvantaged from a life spent in Texas. That is just a plain, undisputed fact. Which is to say, make gumbo every cold Saturday night and red beans and rice every Monday.

- *Do not under any circumstances add miniature livestock.* At best, minis are a fad; at worst, they will leave you starving when the shit hits the fan. A full-size pig provides a large amount of meat in an astonishingly short amount of time. Not so with potbellies. A farm is not a petting zoo. If you want an animal friend, get a dog.

- *Learn to sketch.* Start drawing site plans for fencing, outbuildings, orchards, gardens, and treehouses. (Okay, maybe not treehouses, although you do need to allow for a little whimsy in your life.)

- *Take pictures.* Your farm will change daily.

- *Farm tools are essential.* Acquire these sooner rather than later: come-along, logging chain, post-hole digger, post setter, two pairs of fence pliers, chainsaw (or two or three), rock bar, gardening hoes, mattocks, sledgehammer, knives (pocketknives, boning knife, pruning knife, machete), pitchforks (five-tine, four-tine, and the precious, scarce, and most-used three-tine).

- *Buy a gas-powered generator or two.* Living in a remote valley at the end of the utility line, you'll need it sooner or later. A freezer full of meat without electricity is a sad, smelly business.

- *Get very familiar with these terms:* rotational grazing, green manure, grassfed, free range, organic food (or as your great-grandparents called it, food), sheet mulching, fallow, hard work, Aspercreme.

- *Contact your county extension agent.* He or she can and will help. You don't have to know everything.

- *Work with the Natural Resources Conservation Service* to learn and execute smart resource management practices. From erecting a hoop-house to choosing which trees to cut in a woodlot, the NRCS is one of the few federal agencies that help the small farm make improvements. Its services are not a handout; you do the work, and in return you get expert guidance and financial assistance.

- *Go to any and all estate sales.* Well-cared-for farm tools last several lifetimes.

- *Finally, set up a hammock.* You won't ever have time to relax in it, but it will serve as comic relief when you pass it a dozen times a day drenched in sweat.

Good luck, Nephew. You will do fine and find your own way.

"It does seem so pleasant to talk with an old acquaintance who knows what you know. I see so many new folks nowadays who seem to have nei-ther past nor future. Conversation has got to have some root in the past, or else you have got to explain every remark you make, and it wears a person out."—Sarah Orne Jewett

Well, this wasn't going well. The employee had been babbling on for some minutes about how stupid Southerners are, bashing neighbors, co-workers, and everyone who lived within a few miles of her property. Finally, she drew breath long enough for me to make a point. "You do know I'm from the South, don't you?" I waited a few seconds, knowing exactly what was coming next. "Sure," she said, "but you're not really Southern. You are smart."

It would take a long time to unpack the ignorance that lies behind that colossally impolite statement. That I have heard variations on the same theme from dozens, maybe even hundreds, of others about the South in general and the rural South in specific is enlightening. As many thousands during the great pandemic migration rethought their commitment to liv-ing in the suburbs or the city, I've been constantly mulling over what a move to the country might mean for them.

When someone moves to rural America, the South in particular, the fault lines of prejudice are often laid bare. And here I speak of the new-comer's prejudice, much of which is centered in the post-war suburban ideal that you can filter out contact with those who are different from you. Like the Democrats who have jettisoned blue-collar politics because they are uncomfortable associating with workers as a class and wish to trade them in for something different, outlanders who move to the country often ring clear their biases from the first day and dissatisfaction with what they consider their provincial neighbors on the second—as if the people whose family has lived on the land across the road for four generations could be taken back to the Lexus dealer for a new and more comfortable model.

For those considering a big move "back to the land," tuck this piece of advice in alongside your cultural baggage and worldly goods: Prepare to be lonely, at least until you have demonstrated an old-fashioned liberal willingness to accept people as they are rather than as you wish them to be. It is an age-old fault of humanity, holding up the exotic or at the very least the quaint and the picturesque as more desirable, more noble than the mundane. The reality seldom meets the dream.

Your new neighbor is unlikely to be an Amish farmer who plows with horses, conveniently providing a pastoral backdrop for your Instagram shares. Nope, he is going to be a part-time Primitive Baptist preacher, prone to washing feet on Sunday and voting for "the other candidate" on Tuesday. He is going to gut deer in his front yard. His very existence is going to affront your Peace Corps beliefs, and it sure won't provide your cultural mining more than a meager payout for social media posts.

Yet that same man can weld your broken bushhog (but will take offense when you offer payment). He'll show up and help you mend a fence when your friends in the city only wish to text their assistance. His kids will look after your animals if you're called away, and his whole family will look after you when one of your family members is called home. Just don't—and this is important—open your mouth to tell him how you did things back in Orlando or Ann Arbor.

Still thinking about that move? Let us do a final check, making sure that you are not that sad, clueless, insulting individual about to move to the country but looking to find a different rural population from the one you are going to get. Start by asking yourself a question. Would you really move to rural Thailand and expect to find the cultural options, the governmental services, and the same people you get in a hip Upper West Side New York neighborhood? If that is the case, then you'd better prepare for a life of loneliness. Or, better yet, stay put.

Or, and let me just toss this out as an option, learn to embrace an actual, nonacademic notion of "diversity." The choice is yours. And who knows what you might discover.

8

Compline

IT'S THE FINAL OFFICE, and I'm seated in the doorway of the hoop-house. Behind me the compline bell rings with each shake of the ram's head. The flock is bedded in the barn for the night but still restless. Through the far door of the greenhouse, in the dimming light, the pigs gather as hungry penitents, hoping to be favored by an overgrown turnip or some other toothsome gift. Mere feet away a rabbit munches a cabbage leaf, unconcerned by my presence.

The hour of compline begins with the restless, the hungry, and the insolent . . . which seems to be a certain commentary on something, if I could but grasp it. Meanwhile, in the blue-black sky above, a late jet catches up to the sun's light at 40,000 feet and reflects the granted glory of a temporary membership among the celestial. That too seems to me a lesson, mistaking reflected light as a sign of glory or evidence of mastery. Our species' literature, outside of this current epoch of assumed progressive godhead, is replete with warnings of a fall and our inevitable irrelevance.

We forget the lesson of the Roman triumph, where the servant stood at the conquering general's ear and whispered the message of mortality, or the caution of the young Shelley, that the Ozymandian stature of our achievements is petty compared to the cosmos, or even to a tree, a bee, or a rock.

Perhaps we seek too high for that reflected illumination. Once I had resolved to be as the moon, steadfast in her journey. Now I'm thinking I should be a cabbage. It seems not to care whether rabbit or human eats its leaves; it thrives in that short arc before becoming fodder for whatever destiny.

I laugh out loud at my absurd ruminations, startling the ram out of his own observance. He nervously rings the bell on his collar to close off the hour. Still no closer to an understanding, with this final office now observed, I pick up my chair and turn to leave. The rabbit casts a wary eye, then resumes its predations on my garden.

A final gaze at the night sky before I enter the house finds the familiar winking semaphore still sending its eternal dispatch, which I suspect, if I could just hear, would be whispering in my ear: remember that you are only a man, nothing more.

∗

A farmer's kitchen can be a confusing place for a visitor. Like stumbling into an alchemist's workshop, the guest finds that tied-up bundles of drying herbs hang overhead, bottles filled with colorful liquids steep in the windowsills, and jars whose bulging lids burp malodorous farts sit in the dark corners.

But it's when you open the refrigerator that things become truly strange. A farm fridge is a mysterious place where the acute powers of observation are an essential life skill. Quick, can you spot the difference between the two identical jars, both of which contain a viscous clear liquid? Me neither. Which leads me to ponder, how often over the years have I rid myself of tapeworms while thinking I was merely relaxing with a freshly made Old Fashioned composed of bourbon and my premade simple syrup?

That slightly off-colored liver on the plate on the top shelf? Is it dinner for tonight or an organ sample for the vet to examine postmortem? How many times have I bypassed the homemade ranch dressing and instead retrieved the large jar of milky-white penicillin for the salad? Observation, folks. We begin to see why it so important.

Recently Cindy, having taken advantage of our burgeoning basil patch by making a huge batch of coarsely ground pesto, decided to freeze some of the concoction in ice cube trays. It was one of those Martha Stewart–type innovations that linger unused for years (an observation I kept to myself). A few weeks later, though, recalling her efforts, I determined a little cube of pesto tossed with pasta to be the perfect side to complement a grilled fillet of catfish. I seasoned the fish, started the water boiling for the pasta, and then happened to open the fridge.

Lo and behold, there sat an ice cube-size portion of pesto on a saucer that Cindy had obviously thawed for future use. I pulled it out and left it to finish warming on the counter.

Meanwhile I continued with dinner preparations. I tuned in to a podcast on ancient Greece and poured myself a glass of wine. I fixed the salad, tossed the pasta into the salted boiling water, and put the fish into a skillet to swim in the simmering garlic butter. After the required minutes I drained the pasta and prepared to toss it with the pesto, when at that very moment Cindy came into the kitchen.

Glancing at the pesto on the plate, she said casually, "That fecal sample needs to go back in the fridge. I'm taking it to the vet's in the morning so he can check it for parasites." Timing, as they say, is everything.

Venus is where she should be at six in the morning, fifteen degrees or so above the eastern horizon, shining bright and constant. The dawn is far enough away that the ridgeline is just visible against the hint of a rising light. Just over my shoulder Mars keeps Diana company in watching as her charge wanes to three-quarters. So I sit, drinking my coffee in the early hours with love, war, and the huntress—the only ones with the power to fight off the coming day, at least for another hour.

Making my way to my usual perch this fine Sunday, I passed through a fresh pile of dirt on the walkway behind the house, evidence that one of the dogs had yet again destroyed a thriving raised bed in search of prey or a cool sleeping spot. No bother. Work awaits, of all sorts, for later. Predawn hours spent in simple reflection, staring at the sky and the earth, are my time for renewal, with no agenda or notepad.

Crickets are fiddling in a last mad attempt to attract their one true love. A bullfrog in the stock pond near the massive white oak adds a bass note to the tune, while every few minutes the cock o' the walk in the chicken run voices his approval of the amorous. (The cockerels being fattened for slaughter in a smaller run hold their peace, for now.)

There are no cars this early in the day. Although a state highway, our road is but a winding two-lane and a quarter-mile from the house, so the noise of any traffic is only a minor background hum even at high tide, when our numbers flood over the land in pursuit of work and play. No mowers, no chainsaws, no other of the usual indicators signal that any but I and the overhead power lines are awake.

I sit, churched alone, until inevitably two of the dogs come around the corner, having been alerted through sixth sense to my silent presence. They accept the fact without alarm that I have somehow materialized and take up watch next to my chair. We sit and listen together. A few more minutes and the cat joins the reverie. The light has grown incrementally, and the mood starts to shift as the gods begin to weaken their hold on me, the land, and the sky.

I hear one persistent cricket in the nearby field, clinging to the never-ending search that brings us all into this world. Only after a few more moments of reflection do I come to understand that this cricket, alone, is the clicking of the electric fence, pulsing and popping in the wet grass.

Now my mind begins to think of the day ahead. Sensing the change, the dogs shift from my side and bolt in pursuit of a groundhog reluctant to leave the loaded muscadine vines. My list, which I haven't been aware of until now, grows by another task. The time is here to harvest not only muscadines but also figs. Both are plump and ready for the plucking. I'll also undertake making my annual whole-fig preserves. On a cool night come fall they will be served as an accompaniment to a dinner of gumbo made with one of the fattened cockerels that have now begun to crow in the new day's light.

Draining my cup, I rise and give a nod to Venus. We will dally again, I tell her. Heading back into the house (for it is time to get on with the chores), I leave her to await the coming of her morning consort over the eastern horizon.

Ah, the quality of life for a rooster. From the first creaky pubescent crow to the full-throated voicing that stakes his territory, the rooster rules the roost. That is, if he's the dominant male in the flock. The other suitors lurk in the wings, watching impatiently for the opportunity of a quick assignation in the bushes with a willing (or unwilling) partner. But such is a dangerous existence for the youngster; infringements into the life of the royal court if he's caught in a dalliance can result in a bloody beatdown by the king.

These roosters-in-waiting, these prince regents, skirt the edges of the demesne hoping for an early departure of their paternal unit. The age-old tale of one such rooster is what this story is about: the glorious reign of the heir, elevated at last to the throne . . . if only for a forty-eight-hour period before being toppled by his own lusts.

Our protagonist in this story was a yearling cockerel, one of eight "spares" of his sex who had been caught, separated, and penned for fattening and butcher. From the beginning he stood out as a particularly fine-looking princeling, buff and ready for whatever life might offer. For forty-five days he lived in this all-boys dormitory, one with plenty of outside space in which to quarrel with his mates and then dine twice daily on rich rations. Such was his life, lived in indolence while plumping up for the slaughter, waiting unawares for that cold, cruel day.

Yet, miraculously, on the fateful morning of beheading, he was spared. At the last second, as Cindy wrangled the roosters, handing each to me for the killing cone, we decided on a reprieve for one and only one bird. Our old rooster, a large, beautifully plumed fellow of three years, was chosen for the sacrificial altar in place of the handsome prince. The rex of the roost had lived a good life. But now, in the twilight of his reign, it was time to "counsel" him to abdicate in favor of a younger ruler with a little more pep in his stride.

I grabbed the old boy as he ogled a nice plump hen and unceremoniously dispatched him before adding him to the nine bodies waiting to be plucked and eviscerated. The heir to the throne was released without a formal coronation. Now the only cock of the walk, with twenty females all to himself, the new monarch wasted no time sprinting from hen to hen, fulfilling his destiny (and no doubt his adolescent dreams).

Meanwhile we got on with the work of preparing the carcasses for the freezer. As we cut them open one by one, we noted that their body cavities were filled with fat, hearts covered in globs of glistening yellow, the result of a high-protein-and-grain diet and no occasion to be chased by a ruling rooster and burn it off—all of which would make for some mighty tasty soups and gumbos (though, had they lived, not so much for good cardio-health and a long and active lifestyle). We gave it no more thought.

Two days later I walked out to the sawmill beyond the hay barn. There I found the newly crowned king dead on the ground—death by heart attack, no doubt brought on by a frantic forty-eight hours of lusty indulgence as he made up for lost time trying to satisfy all the hens in his domain.

And that should have been the end of this tale of a farm without a rooster, except . . . except that a few days later we discovered another handsome cockerel. He had bided his time even farther out on the fringes of the dominion, lying in wait for this momentous day. Now he has returned to his ancestral lands and claimed the throne, this heir-and-a-spare, and having eaten heart-healthy all his life, he leads (we hope) a somewhat more enduring existence as ruler of the roost.

There are days when the feeling of being a relic of another age haunts my every step. Such was the case last night, when while looking for a recipe for fried catfish I discovered a letter, tucked into the pages of a cookbook, from an old friend. Instead of preparing dinner I caught up with the 2011 version of my friend in her small village in Norfolk, England.

I could just as easily have grabbed my copy of Irvine Welsh's *Trainspotting* and read the tucked-away letter of 1996 from my decades-long friend who lives in London, in which he provided a translation of slang to help me understand the novel. Or I could have chanced upon the lengthy letter from my dear uncle, now deceased, from January 1981, following my visit from Lake Charles to see him and his wife, my aunt, in Knoxville over Christmas 1980. Among the hundreds of books in my library reside dozens that hold the ephemera of my life.

This habit of longstanding, the placing of letters and postcards received into books selected at random, rewards. It gives me renewed emotional connections to people I know and love, knew and loved. This habit shared by many is the reason that out-of-print bookstore owners carefully leaf through the pages of books as they purchase: to find those records of life (and the occasional currency) that, in the sellers' case, add value to the book.

It is also one of the reasons booksellers prefer the well-worn book to the newly printed title. Those old books are sanctified, bathed in the blood of time, and they share a permanent kinship with the former owners. Out of a biography of William Morris I once purchased fell an invoice dated July 23, 1926, from Mayhew Second-hand Booksellers on Charing Cross Road, London. That I had an invoice from that road, so well-known among bibliophiles (84 Charing Cross Road), to a woman living in Knoxville, Tennessee, was a miraculous connection. I would like to have known her and why she ordered that title from that shop.

There is a cultural value to ephemera, whether it's a postcard addressed to me or an invoice tucked away in a book or a bundle of letters nestled beside a faded sachet in a dressing table drawer. Ephemera connect us all. If not for the practitioners of writing and saving letters I would not now have the correspondence of my father to his mother, written while he was stationed in the Pacific during World War II. I would not have the letter (found in a book belonging to my grandmother) from a great-great aunt to my great-grandmother complaining of getting fat from drinking beer in her old age. By losing the ephemera, we lose the moments of serendipity that go with them.

The overall decline in literacy—a drum I play often—will no doubt have its detrimental effect. But so too will the overall loss of curiosity about our past that this minor act of historical mining encourages. Why would we be interested in the letters of an aunt or uncle, found in a book, if we don't read books in the first place? Why would we write a letter when we care only about digital bytes of information, or simply reject the past in all of its parts in favor of the self-chosen family of the present? For the uninquisitive, the aliterate, the presentist, the past is opaque, perhaps never having even occurred. The life of the email, the text, the tweet, the Instagram picture, all are ephemeral, each instantly deletable.

While this digital infatuation may be the enemy of future scholars, it is our collective loss as well. To experience the genuine pleasure of opening a book and having a letter fall into your lap, leaving you to spend a few minutes or an evening recalling a friend, a loved one, even a stranger, and for a moment in time to step out of the present, is to connect with the past that we shouldn't give up.

When you are deep in the winter mud season it is hard to see through to the other side, where spring rules. Could I but string two intimate days with the sun, no rain, and a warming wind, then I'm sure my mood would lift. But each day, this day, I slog. I slog out to the barn to feed the sheep. I slog to the chicken coop. I slosh and slog to feed the pigs, raising with each step a black-brown slurry that splatters my newly laundered Carhartts. Looking down with disgust, I turn to find something convenient to kick, and sink ankle-deep into the mire.

I stomp back to the house to change my clothes. Once inside, I do a compulsive check of the weather website. I shout upstairs to Cindy, "It's going to be cloudy and rainy today." "Yeah, I'm looking out the window," she replies to the idiot who seeks digital confirmation of the obvious.

Having failed to receive appropriate commiseration, I review my impressively detailed to-do list. It doesn't take much searching to find an excuse to do nothing. Listed on the page is a multitude of tasks related to mud season . . . none of which can be completed because it is mud season.

We need a dump truck of fill dirt delivered to redirect rain runoff from pooling in the inner corral, but the driver wants a guarantee he won't get stuck in the mud. Which means that maybe in July, when the sludge of winter is a dim memory and I trudge through my rounds cursing the heat and drought of summer, he will show up.

Then there is the large pile of gravel to be distributed where the sheep traverse gates and buildings, areas where the mud is deepest. Yet the tractor in this season slips and slides with alarming imprecision as I navigate the entryways, and the front tires sink deep into the mud when I attempt to pick up the heavy load of gravel. It's another task that must wait for summer (when all the time in the world will be allotted to winter tasks, no doubt).

Which reminds me of an essay I wrote in third grade:

"I just finished my last math test and now am taking my last writing test. Things don't look very good right now. But soon it will all be over, and I can run and jump and fish and play."

I like that kid, I think. He certainly had his priorities straight.

I head back outside to work in the hoop-house. At the far end of the barnyard, through various muck-laden gates, the hoop-house in winter is a delight, both warmish and dry. What water there is comes from a drip tape that irrigates the rows in a controlled fashion. Unless, that is, one of the tapes breaks. That's when you open the door to find that your well-organized watering overnight (for the past eight hours) has created a muddy mess that mirrors the world outside. Sadly, and not surprisingly, on this day, that is exactly the picture the open door reveals.

Soon it will all be over, and then I can run and jump.

No matter what kind of trouble a teenage boy might get into on a Friday night, he will be home in time to raid the fridge for a midnight snack. It is a plain and simple fact of nature: home is where the stomach gets filled, as the adage goes (or should).

Of all the skills we have learned on the farm (and we have learned plenty in twenty-some years), among the first and most critical lessons in Husbandry 101 is the importance of hollering for dinner. Teach your livestock to come to feed, and your life has been made much easier. Call them even when they're confined to a barn. Let them associate your bellow with getting fed. They will love you for it.

Yes, stepping out into a field for the first time and hollering for cattle with neighbors in earshot makes you feel like a right idiot. Get over it. I have been with friends who struggled with controlling their livestock. The reason was clear. As the herd ran rampant over distant fields, said friends would stand in the barn doorway with a bucket and say at a near-whisper, "Here, cattle. Come here, cattle," then shake the bucket like it was filled with feathers that were about to float away.

You can't pussyfoot around—you have to call your livestock like you mean it. Start by getting them used to a little feed every day. When we first bring in a load of weanling pigs, we keep them confined for twenty-four hours. Each time they get fed, even though they are five feet away, we holler, "Here piggee, piggee, piggeeee!" (The classic "Sooey!" used to call pigs is said to derive from the Latin *Suidae*, the family that includes domestic hogs.)

Walking out to the barn at sunset and giving a holler, "Here chick, chick, chick!" and then watching the chickens, heads down and at a fast waddle, stream from all points of the compass, or being under the gun to treat a lamb for scours and shaking a bucket and blasting out a booming "Come on, girls; come on!" and having fifty ewes and lambs stampede toward you from 400 yards away—those immediate responses to your call are more than just satisfying. They're critical.

Pigs, I will note, are not sheep or cattle or chickens. They are notoriously unreliable and often downright obstinate. They will come running if still confined to their paddock. But if they have escaped, slightly different rules apply. They may if hungry (and pigs, like boys, are almost always hungry) follow your cries and a bucket of feed back to hearth and home. Or they may ignore you (in which case they will typically return overnight, homed in on the trough of feed, unless, of course, they don't). Regardless, recapture is more easily done when any stock have been handled and when they associate the sound of your distinctive call with safety and feed.

Last night several couples joined us for a St. Paddy's dinner celebration. Shortly after arriving one of the couples told us of seeing a flock of sheep out on the road a couple of miles away. Cindy and the couple went to assist. Turns out the farmer was out of state and unable to help. Twenty-odd lambs had already scattered every which direction, and only a flock of eight greeted Cindy, our guests, and one other neighbor. It was apparent those lambs had never been "called to dinner" or even left their barnyard. How much more smoothly things would have gone if with a simple holler of "Come on, girls" and the rattle of a bucket they had turned toward home. As it was, after forty minutes of coaxing lambs toward their barn half a mile away and vehicles stacking up on the country road, Cindy and guests turned and headed home for their own dinner, leaving the job in the hands of the newly gathered reinforcements to finish.

Was it a coincidence that we who had stayed at the farm had just stepped out onto the porch and yelled, "Come on, Cindy. Come on"?

Remembering Becky: Where I enter the woods near the wet-weather spring the ground is moist and spongy underfoot. The air is cool, so different from the oven-like summer day left a few feet back. The lane as it curves up into the woods dips and then rises gradually up the long slope of the ridge. Our English shepherd Becky weaves back and forth in the brush following her own invisible road of smells and other enticements.

Leaving the lane I begin my own weave in the woods, not her scent-driven journey but no less purposeful for that. Boletes and milk caps carpet the floor, sprung into being after a recent rain. It's an act of creation far removed from the act of wielding buzzing saws in the next valley, where a son is clear-cutting the wooded inheritance left by his father—an act, I imagine, completed with the same quiet understanding and betrayal of the sons in the final pages of Pearl S. Buck's *The Good Earth*.

Looking for a flush of chanterelles, or at least enough to accompany dinner, I find only two. I am now in the middle of the woods, where sounds entering are muted and filtered, sanitized of offense. A doe jumps and runs away with an exaggerated slowness. I know that dance. She has left a fawn in the brush and leads Becky far away before easily eluding her. Nearby I spot the bright rust and white spots of the sleeping fawn, no more than twenty pounds, unaware of her mother's exertions.

I have now come to the fence at the base of the ridge, newly installed last year. A large branch has already fallen, crushing the wire to the ground. Shifting the branch, I repair the wire with my fence pliers, each strand crimped back into tight harmony with the whole. Becky and I walk the perimeter until we get to the gates between the upper pasture and the hopper field. I pull the gate closed and latch it. I'll move the cattle in a few days and have come on this walk to make the pasture secure.

We emerge from the shade of the trees and cross the pasture. Becky plunges into the dew pond to cool off, sending a dozen bullfrogs plopping from shore into the depths. I'm sweating as we reenter the woods. The details of the remaining to-do list begin to crowd in as we walk back down the lane. Becky, no longer chasing scents, senses the change and stays by my side.

The woods now seem a bit stifling as the mid-afternoon sun drives all thought of breeze away. We retrace our path through the pasture back to the barn. In the barnyard Becky dives for the shade under the chicken coop. I linger for a few minutes and then follow her example and head to the house for a nap.

Becky first arrived on our farm after a long flight from South Dakota. It was May 2008, and she was nine weeks old. I let her out of the truck, and she immediately climbed the steps onto the porch, then turned around and growled at the two large adult dogs, Tip and Robby, who came to greet her. "Don't come up on *my* front porch," she seemed to be saying. I laughed. Good working farm dogs have both grit and intelligence. This dog clearly had both.

The following month ushered in calving season. A first-time mother had given birth the day before to a heifer somewhere in the ten-acre field above the house. Now she had managed to lose track of her calf and stood at the top of the hill and bawled, staring down, waiting for us to do something. Cindy saddled her Morgan mare and began the search for the missing newborn. For a few minutes Becky and I stayed in the backyard watching. Then it was just me. Becky had slipped under the gate and disappeared into the five acres of woods adjoining the pasture. The bawling cow, meanwhile, followed behind Cindy as she crisscrossed the upper fence line a few hundred yards away.

That's when it happened. Within five minutes of having slipped under the gate, Becky—not yet four months old—emerged from the woods, weaving back and forth behind a newborn calf, pushing it forward into the pasture. At the top of the field the mother quickly caught sight. She gave a great bellow and galumphed down to her calf, immediately nudging her back to the business end to nurse. To this day I get chills when I tell the story. That was the complete farm dog package on display: work ethic, instinct, and a level of intelligence several notches above that of your average human teenager.

A working farm dog is a companion, certainly. More important, it is a partner. Sending a dog out of earshot and having it bring in a flock of sheep or locate an injured animal; watching the dog move a half-ton recalcitrant steer in a tight chute, occasionally getting kicked but always going back to get the job done; standing by as the dog puts just enough pressure on a protective ewe with a newborn to guide her into a lambing pen without charging—if you haven't seen or experienced any of this, then you are missing out on one of the great satisfactions in life.

Becky had the run of the farm, day and night. During the day she was our right hand. At night she took on raccoons, opossums, skunks, foxes, and coyotes to keep the property varmint- and predator-free. She spent her whole life outside, except for her morning ritual. When I got up, made coffee, then let the other dogs off the back porch, Becky would be by the back door waiting to be let in for her "quiet time." She would stay inside for thirty minutes and then stand near the door to be let out.

She was uniformly loved by people and feared by other dogs; she never met another of her kin that she didn't wish to (and sometimes did) rip into. The only thing she was afraid of was thunder, until, that is, the last couple of years, when her hearing diminished to the point that a rumble no longer affected her.

The life of the working farm dog is a tough one, and all of those hard days and hard knocks eventually catch up. But even as her health failed, in spite of being mostly blind and deaf and severely arthritic, even as ultimately she struggled to stand, Becky still did her part. During her last week she helped move our flock of ewes and held off the rams while we were feeding.

When Becky lapsed into semi-consciousness at the age of fourteen, suffering from various ailments, we had her euthanized. We buried her in the garden next to her old workmates, Robby and Tip. The next morning I awoke thinking about how to remember her. I went downstairs and made coffee, then let out our two pet dogs, Max and Buster. Becky, of course, was not waiting at the back door. I did not call her name during the day to help. She did not sit next to my chair on the porch, within easy reach, occasionally pushing her head under my hand to remind me to pet her.

The farm had changed. The sheep now do as they wish, the rams invade our space, a calf remains hidden, and stray dogs remain unmolested. We miss our Becky.

Buster stands hypnotized as our aged cat, Chip, gingerly crosses the porch. It is five o'clock, still pitch dark, and the rat terrier is on high alert: "If I squint just right that could be a giant rat." I call his name and the spell is broken. We—dogs, cat, and I—resume our predawn reverie in peace. A little drizzle is just beginning to fall in what is forecast to be a rainy Sunday. Which reminds me that I never did clean the gutters. It's a task usually remembered when the rainwater is overflowing along the whole of the roof's little canal.

I've come outside with my coffee hoping to be favored with the pulsing din of the cicadas. In spring and summer of 2004 we sat out most evenings until late into the night, not talking, letting the deafening chorus envelop us. But this morning, like last evening, like all season, it is quiet. Friends report the emergence of Brood X in Blount, two counties away. Here in Roane there are only the usual sounds of birds, crickets, a few echoing roosters up and down the valley, and the bass of a bullfrog setting the rhythm in the backyard pond.

Beyond today's gutter cleaning, my mental list of what needs doing is short. Depending on the rain, I need to finish the garlic harvest. Yesterday I pulled up all the red onions and half the garlic and laid them out on tables in the barn to cure before storing them under the stairs in the house for future use. I also finished cutting up two felled trees and tossed the logs into the bed of the old farm truck, where they'll probably stay until the truck is required for something else. Late in the morning the Kid and I walked up and down hills disassembling the electric fence and restringing it elsewhere, a task we do most Saturdays as part of the routine of rotating pasture for the sheep.

The newest Kid continues to work out well. He tackles the farm chores if not with finesse then with gusto. Other than hand-weeding, that is. It is a fact universally acknowledged that a thirteen-year-old boy doesn't want the piddly tasks. Experience (and I speak here with authority gleaned from dim personal recollection) has taught that he wants the sweaty, testosterone-pumping, tear-into-it, get-'er-done kind of work. This is great for the farm, because we always have plenty of those jobs to do. Yesterday the Kid and I tore into it and got 'er done, which today leaves me in an exertion-avoidance mode.

Maybe some kraut- or kimchi-making is in the pipeline for this afternoon? The garden is loaded with cabbages. It is time to prepare them for our own use or feed them to the pigs, the snails, and the fluttering cabbage whites. Everyone gets to eat on this farm.

Yesterday morning I was in the gardens by six, feeling giddy at the start of the day. I had that goofy, grin-on-the-face feeling that all is right with the world if one lives in East Tennessee on a small farm with a full day ahead. Many days are like that, most even. That the day ended with our sitting on the back deck enjoying a dinner of steaks, salad, new blue potatoes, and grilled asparagus and spring onions solidified my first impression. The only thing that could have improved a perfect day was for the sun to have set to the accompaniment of serenading cicadas seeking love.

The leaves begin to thin imperceptibly at the start of October, the pace quickening as the month passes until one powerful storm, often the first week or two of November, scatters all to the ground. In their leaving, stark shapes out of myth and folklore will walk the forest, stand as watchful sentinels in the middle of a pasture. It is a beautiful transformation.

While each month is an ending, in fall and winter we feel it most keenly. Spring and summer, by contrast, are seasons of abundance, filled with work that is characterized by restraining the energies of nature, channeling it for productive needs that we desire. Spring and summer are a time of growth, wild and teenaged, that without pruning (and sometimes with) overwhelms. Their days are filled with hours of sowing and planting, mowing and harvesting. Sunlight lingers deep into the evening, long after the will to do more has flagged.

Then the seasons turn. Starting with the falling of the leaves, the farm shifts to maintaining and maintenance. There is new life still—garlic and onions planted in October, lambing midwinter, greens in the hoop-house, potatoes sown in February. But the time has come for clearing fencerows, cutting back old-growth vines and spent plants, repairing hay barns and other outbuildings.

Now begins the practical time of the year, less driven by the ever-present struggle to keep up and more molded by the rarer opportunity to catch up. Which is perhaps why farmers traditionally speak of fall and winter as slower. The workload doesn't lessen, but the character of the labor changes fundamentally. It is more structural, both literally and figuratively; with hands to the saw and mind released from the routine and endless sunlight, the farmer can focus more on the process and life.

That my father passed away three weeks ago and my stepmother joined him last night finds me a bit more introspective than usual this season. Farming has shifted my appreciation and understanding of the cycles of life; it also, I hope, has made me more accepting of certain inevitable changes that life brings to us all. It has, and I hope this is understood, made me appreciate more deeply the devoted care that my two sisters in Lake Charles gave to both parents over the past eight years. To my way of thinking they husbanded well their charges, with attention and love, then let them go graciously when the time arrived.

That both parents departed as summer ended and fall began is a gift to use, one that can shape the work to come: help me mend what I have and prepare for the new life that while already growing dormant is also readying for rebirth.

Our farm occasions a lot of queries from observers drawn to what appears to be a bucolic life. We try to answer their questions dutifully, but since they don't farm they have difficulty articulating what they really need to ask. And we seldom tell them the full truth.

What they are really asking is, is the farming life for me? And what I'd like to tell them is this: The simple reality of farming is work, hard physical work. It is work that can't be put off, work that piles up in ever-increasing amounts, overwhelms, floods over every moment of your life, drowns you in immeasurable to-do lists and immeasurable to-dos.

Farming is ninety-eight degrees in July, flat on your back under a piece of equipment in the farthermost field, coated in grease, dry hay in your eyes and down your shirt, with the wrong tool a half-mile away as you try to fix something you knew was ready to break and put off because of all the other things you knew were ready to break and did get fixed, or at least patched together.

Farming is having the flu and a fever, puking, being weak and barely able to stand as you go through your rounds, feeding, hauling water. There are no sick days, and you earn way less than minimum wage just for the pleasure of it. It is throwing out your back or neck or elbow, spraining an ankle, splashing tractor oil in your eye when you live thirty-five minutes from the nearest hospital. It is cutting your own firewood because the utility company hasn't trimmed trees since the last ice storm and the forecast is always for weather you didn't predict. Farming is serving as chief veterinary officer and surgeon because vets no longer make farm visits.

Farming is blood and mud so thick on your clothes and hands that you don't know which is which and whether they are from you, the ground, or the dying animal you've been trying to save. Farming is twelve degrees in January with winds gusts of twenty miles per hour and sleet stinging your face as you try to get a chainsaw to start to cut up the tree that fell across the fence, allowing your herd of cattle to wander the countryside.

Farming is your neighbor's barn burning down due to faulty wiring, which in turn causes you to bump repairing your own faulty barn wiring from No. 375 to No. 1 on the list of this year's tasks. It is a customer so obstinate, so dumb, so plain unthinking that you are tempted to give up the whole enterprise or the human race or maybe both as a bad investment.

Farming is also the intensity of a redbud in spring that stops you in your tracks while all the other miserable sods are trying to stay awake in the office or factory. So achingly beautiful is that redbud that it keeps you rooted in place and doing nothing for the next twenty minutes. Farming is a perfect cone-shaped swarm of honey bees hanging from your peach tree, a swarm that is then easily captured as it drops as a single clump into your waiting hive box.

Farming is the ripe tomato, the hand-milled apple cider, the baskets full of potatoes in cold storage, the ham curing under the stairs, the freezing midnight alone at the top of the hill. It is bees bearding on the front of the hive on a summer day, cutting hay on a Memorial Day weekend, admiring a newly erected fence line and knowing intimately the work that went into building it.

Farming is a barn stacked with the hay you just baled, a garden bursting with produce. It is freshly baked bread slathered with the honey that you harvested, hamburgers off the grill courtesy of the lambs you raised on the hillside behind the house, a bowl of homemade yogurt topped with blueberries plucked from the backyard. Farming is the joy of lambing, the loveliness of a newborn calf, the hatching of chicks, the "grin" on the ram as he is released into the flock. It is a randy romp of fecundity from spring through winter. Farming is the birds and the bees, all day and all night.

Farming is the pleasure of doing for yourself, caring for the land, caring for your customers (even *that* one), providing for your family and countless others. Farming is not about you. It is about the vegetables you raise, the livestock you rear, the land you steward, the wildlife you provide shelter for, the satisfaction of being a good tenant on this good earth.

Farming is not a career. It is not a lifestyle. It is life.

Printed in the USA
CPSIA information can be obtained
at www.ICGtesting.com
LVHW010738181023
761402LV00016B/293